'A timely, insightful book about staying creative in a changing world. Using her extensive experience and impressive knowledge, Margaret Heffernan highlights what it takes to excel in turbulent times.'
Adam Grant, author of *Think Again* and *Hidden Potential*, and host of the podcast ReThinking

'A fascinating and thought-provoking read. Margaret Heffernan makes it very clear that, confronted by uncertainty, we need to think like artists. *Embracing Uncertainty* is current, unique in its approach, solid and necessary.'
Penny Hay, Bath Spa University

'A call to creativity, written as a response to the deadening effects of tech-enabled managerialism. This long-overdue book invites readers of whatever stripe to learn from the way artists work, to see uncertainty for what it is: "the great propulsive power behind curiosity, learning, discovery and invention – the essence of being human"'.
Tracey Camilleri, co-author of *The Social Brain*

'At a time when algorithms promise to extinguish all doubt, Heffernan makes a compelling case for uncertainty as humanity's greatest resource. Her deep examination of how artists work offers an inspired and inspiring model for thriving in an unpredictable world.'

Daniel H. Pink, author of *The Power of Regret*, *Drive* **and** *A Whole New Mind*

'There is no more compelling, convincing and articulate guide to what the arts have to teach us about uncertainty than Margaret Heffernan.'

Robert Poynton, author of *Do Improvise*

'Margaret Heffernan's beautifully expressed insight that the essential quality of artistry is a strength we all need and can develop in ourselves is hugely welcome. A life-enhancing book.'

Lucy Parker, co-author of *The Activist Leader* **and Senior Partner at the Brunswick Group**

EMBRACING UNCERTAINTY

How Writers, Musicians and Artists Thrive in an Unpredictable World

Margaret Heffernan

First published in Great Britain in 2025 by

Policy Press, an imprint of
Bristol University Press
University of Bristol
1-9 Old Park Hill
Bristol
BS2 8BB
UK
+44 (0)117 374 6645
bup-info@bristol.ac.uk

Details of international sales and distribution partners are available at
policy.bristoluniversitypress.co.uk

British Library Cataloguing in Publication Data
A catalogue record for this book is available from the British Library

ISBN 978-1-4473-7267-7 paperback
ISBN 978-1-4473-7268-4 ePub
ISBN 978-1-4473-7269-1 ePdf

Cover design: Mecob

Bristol University Press and Policy Press use environmentally
responsible print partners.

Printed in and bound in Great Britain by CPI Group (UK) Ltd,
Croydon CR40 4YY

FSC
www.fsc.org
MIX
Paper | Supporting
responsible forestry
FSC® C013604

For Roy and Aisling

Contents

List of figures

List of figures

Acknowledgements

This book came about largely due to enthusiastic, creative people who paid attention to an argument I was making and thought there might be more to it: Mary Ward-Lowery and Matthew Dodd, who commissioned the original talks for BBC Radio 3's *The Essay*, and Ginny Mills, who heard them – thank you for noticing.

Everyone interviewed in this book was open and generous in giving me precious time and not bridling too much at my questions; thank you for yours. I hope I've represented you truthfully but don't expect you to agree with everything I've written.

As I explain in this book, all creative work comes out of a concatenation of ideas, observations, conversations and a lot of wandering around. I've had the good fortune to wander with wonderful people – Charlie Aubry, Chris Bagley, Sebastian Barry, the entire Bicat family, Cowboy Blau, Howard Brenton, Chila Kumari Burman, Subir Chowdhury, Janet Cooper, Ciaran Dunne, Sarah Gillard, Jonathan Gosling, Lamin Daniel Jadama, John Keane, Vinod Khosla, Jenny Matthews, Richard Olivier, Victoria Oruwari, Rob Poynton, Susanne Schuler, Pamela Stewart, David Wetherell and Zina Saro-Wiwa have all hugely enriched my thinking in this book. Penny Hay, Andrew Amondson, Andrew Grant and the whole marvellous Forest of Imagination family allowed me to experience first hand the true generosity of artists in their work and their practice. I'm also indebted to Maggie Jackson's wonderful book on the neuroscience of uncertainty, which brought some biology to the bones of my argument.

I'm grateful to Oliver Evans at the Maureen Paley gallery and to Matthew Flowers of Flowers Gallery for helping me to understand better the career and gallery structure that supports and encourages their artists. If it weren't for Matthew, I would never have encountered DACS (Design and Artists Copyright Society), the collecting society for visual artists from whose staff, members and board members I have learned so much; thank you especially to Cedar Lewisohn who introduced me to street art and to Julia Crabtree who always reminded me that artists have bills to pay. The DACS team do phenomenal work for an excellent cause with great spirit. I'm also grateful to Gilane Tawadros for introducing me to the brilliant work of Frank Bowling.

Thanks are due to Clare Carlisle who first set me on the path of thinking about politics and the arts when she invited me to lecture on the subject at King's College, London. Caryl Phillips has been a lifelong source of inspiration and friendship. I could never have talked to so many generous and provocative artists without Andy Pemberton and the inspiration of his wife Dionne McCulloch. Thank you for saving my bacon! Juliet Blake seems to believe in me when I don't, and to know what I'm talking about when I don't, and I still don't quite know why, but am ever grateful.

I'm indebted to both Bath Spa University and the University of Bath, both of which have supported my ideas and my work in multiple ways. It's fascinating sitting at the crossroads where an arts university and a science university meet (or don't!). I have also been fortunate to see how Oxford's Saïd Business School is stretching the agenda for executive education – in Tracey Camilleri, Sam Rockey and Lucy Shaw they have some true pioneers. I appreciate all my colleagues at Merryck & Co, who have shown me how receptive the business community can be to the arts – far more than is commonly assumed. I also value the insights I've gained from the business leaders I'm lucky enough to work with, individuals who face uncertainty daily.

Much of this book was inspired by watching the early years of emerging artists, their struggles and their determination. I'm deeply grateful to my children for reminding me that the most interesting point of an artistic career is not always at the end. Felix Nicholson, Leonora Nicholson, Pauline Payen and Lana Harris are tough, kind, endlessly inventive artists in their own right, and I'm frequently in awe of their nerve and determination.

Two people make my chaotic life manageable. The first is Stephanie Cooper-Lande, who always seems to roll with the punches and not take mishaps too seriously. Thank you for your endless patience. My agent Natasha Fairweather is clear-headed and forthright, and I am always grateful for her astute advice.

As for my husband Lindsay, he doesn't need a book to know how uncertain book writing is, but has shown an exceptional capacity for patience, endurance and enthusiasm beyond imagining.

Finally this book is dedicated to Roy and Aisling Foster. Both artists in their own right: in their work, in their friendships, in their delicacy and generosity. From them I learned that it is our friends that keep us alive. Friends and art.

Farrington Gurney, 2025

Prologue:
the cost of certainty

'The train will arrive in 2 minutes.' About 20 years ago, as I stood on a train platform hearing that announcement, a thought experiment flashed through my mind.

On waking, I go to my wardrobe where clothes have already been selected for the damp British day. Everything I want for breakfast is stocked in my fridge. Confident I won't need a raincoat, I wait just a minute or two for the bus, knowing it will be on time. It takes me to a health check that was scheduled just before I got sick. I know this, with the same confidence that I'm sure to arrive on time, as will the doctor. I understand the nature of the illness and I'm calm, certain my treatment will prove successful. My company has already booked me out for the time required for my recovery. During that time, my fridge will continue to be automatically restocked with healthy foods, and anything else I need will be on tap. The days are frictionless, everything is convenient. The shape of the years to come, the friends I will make and the ones I'll lose, the books I will read and the places I will go: all of this I know right up to, and including, the day that I will die.

All uncertainty in my life has gone.

• • •

When I share this thought experiment, at first people are delighted by the novelty of the bus arriving on time. But as the certainty mounts, their delight turns to horror. Life reveals itself as one giant 'To do' list – being alive consists merely of crossing things off. Financial planning might get easier, but being a passenger in the journey of one's own life doesn't feel like life at all.

That initial response to the experiment is always telling: the idea of having all aspects of life under control is alluring, for the simple reason that uncertainty is stressful. If I don't know when my partner will get home from work, I worry that we won't get to the cinema in time, we could miss dinner, and risk annoying the friends we are due to meet there. A whole concatenation of consequences can spool out in my mind before I've even asked the question. Whatever answer I get still contains contingencies: leaving the office early offers no guarantee of a punctual arrival. What if the bus is cancelled? A trivial vignette of daily life reveals the chasm of uncertainty that is a defining characteristic of human life.

We make decisions all the time. Important and trivial ones – who to marry, whether to have children, what to eat, what to wear – and we want to be sure they are right, or at least the best they can be. But really each is just a hypothesis about a future we don't know, because it hasn't happened yet. We can't skip to the last chapter in the book of our lives and sneak a peek to see how it all ends up. So we worry. And we'd prefer not to.

Managers are paid to worry. 'Imagine Westminster under water', Sam Woods, head of the Bank of England's Prudential Regulation Authority, surmises. He knows that extreme weather events are happening all over the world. What would it mean for markets if a major financial hub – London, Paris, New York – were knocked out? It would be irresponsible not to design a scenario to test the consequences of such an event that is clearly feasible and would have a big impact on government and markets. Would there be mortgage defaults, bankruptcies, lawsuits, stranded assets? But merely asking the questions proliferates uncertainty. How might businesses react when they are warned? What if they're not? What if no such event ever occurs? Unknowns compound.[1] Woods, even with vast resources at his command, lives our daily quandary.

At work, at home, we think about the future all the time. Competing scenarios do battle in our minds – eat earlier, see the film later, cancel the friends and go alone, don't go at all! – triggering the release of noradrenaline, a hormone that increases attention and alertness. The brain consumes a lot of energy, furiously trying to resolve the conflicts. This is the physical reality of stress. Too much uncertainty provokes hypervigilance, as though the brain has experienced trauma.[2] No wonder the promise of certainty can be so seductive.

How far we'd go to achieve certainty became visible in experiments that date from the 1970s, in which volunteers were subjected to electric shocks delivered by a machine. The critical detail is that these were emitted randomly; at any moment a shock might come, or it might not; they might occur more frequently, or stop altogether. For many people in the experiments, not knowing what would happen next became so intolerable that they seized control to deliver the shocks to themselves. They preferred certain, controlled pain to the uncomfortably ambiguous position of waiting to find out whether the pain would stop or recur.[3] A similar but more recent study showed that participants with just a 50 per cent chance of receiving a shock experienced more stress than those who knew with 100 per cent certainty that they would be shocked.[4] Guaranteed pain was preferable to uncertain suffering. Similarly, when neuroscientists studied volunteers who were given a time estimation test, they discovered that some participants preferred feedback that was blunt and wholly negative to a more subtle, ambiguous commentary – they would rather be confident they'd failed than linger to wonder, hope or interpret.[5]

Studies like these illustrate how stressful not knowing can be and how far we may go in search of certainty. So it's no wonder that allaying our anxiety is big business: not just anxiolytics, but warranties, insurance policies and apps. GPS reassures us we will get to the cinema on time, dating apps promise we will like the blind date, Tripadvisor reassures us that the hotel will be clean and that the restaurant will be great. Ratings and rankings perform a similar service: that school may be a long walk but it's worth it; that university is bound to land you a great job. We've been persuaded that data is the source of all certainty, even though GPS can't tell in advance if the car in front of me is about to break down, dating apps can't know in which details my date might not have been entirely truthful, how exorbitant my standard of cleanliness is or how eccentric my food preferences. With more ignorance than knowledge about me, what comfort I derive from such services can only ever be probabilistic: likely, but still not certain. The irony is that they may induce as much stress as they purport to reduce – where once I made social plans, confident my friends would stick to them, now I check my phone over and over again to make sure nothing has gone wrong. As my expectations have increased, so too has my need for reassurance.

For technology companies, our allergy to uncertainty has become a goldmine. 'For individuals, the attraction [sic] is the possibility of a world where everything is arranged for your convenience – your health check-up is magically scheduled just as you begin to get sick, the bus comes just as you get to the bus stop, and there is never a line of waiting people at city hall.' This is Alex Pentland's thought experiment; you can imagine my surprise when I encountered it in an academic paper.[6] What I felt to be dystopian he presented as compelling, manifest destiny. Pentland ran MIT's Media Lab, is an entrepreneur, and has worked extensively for Google. His premise is apparently simple enough: with enough sensors, robotics and computing power, you can get buses, books and food to arrive on time. Those systems are easily controllable; it's people who introduce uncertainty. But given enough data and good enough predictive models of human behaviour, it should be possible to produce what he calls 'social efficiency' – a planned society that keeps everyone and everything on the right track. And it's a business model he thinks worth plugging.

This utopian promise is, on one level, typical Silicon Valley propaganda: selling tech dependency to anxious people craving certainty. The mindset is deeply informed by 70 years of behaviourism, a branch of psychology whose goal is the prediction and control of human behaviour. Aspiring to the same rigour as physics, its central tenet is that every human action and decision is a response to stimuli. Once you have enough data with which to model behaviour, you can stop people doing the wrong things by incentivizing (or nudging) them to do the right thing. That's the way to eliminate uncertainty and keep everyone happy. Or at least compliant.

B.F. Skinner, the founding father of behaviourism, lamented that while the science of physics had taken us to the moon, human development had severely lagged behind. Citing an urgent need to eliminate poverty, ignorance, overconsumption and 'unchecked breeding', it was time for scientists to 'fix' human behaviour.[7] He felt the solution was nearly within his grasp;

4

with sufficient experimental data and computing power, he felt confident of developing a 'technology of behaviour' that would analyse, predict and then be able to adjust how we behave for the greater good.[8] It's not so very different from a current popular psychologist who once exclaimed to me, 'We've seen the enemy – and it's us! And we are going to fix it!'

Skinner had no time for unmeasurable concepts like agency and autonomy; these, he argued, were just stories we told ourselves to justify choices that were only reactions to, or against, stimuli. There is no such thing as an inner life. In his 1971 book *Beyond Freedom and Dignity*, Skinner insisted that such ideas are as ridiculous and archaic as Aristotle's belief that falling bodies move because they are so happy to be going home. Imagining a future in which his vision was achieved, Skinner gloated, 'It is the autonomous inner man who is abolished, and that is a step forward.'

Pentland's concept of 'social physics' takes behaviourism one step further, arguing that, as social creatures, we don't really make our own decisions. Studies on so-called 'social contagion' show how ubiquitously behaviours can spread across a group unconsciously. Obesity, smoking, divorce and depression proliferate across social networks in ways that can be mathematically modelled.[9] These changes are determined, not chosen: we aren't really making decisions but conforming to the people around us. From a behaviourist's perspective, that is the great news: stimuli scale. Because we are subject to social influence, uncertainty can be reduced by designing rewards that masses of people will respond to in unison. We achieve social efficiency, in effect, by not having to think at all – and that's progress because it's time, Pentland argues with some impatience, 'that we dropped the fiction of individuals as the unit of rationality, and recognised that our rationality is largely determined by the surrounding social fabric.'[10] Since everything that matters is measurable, sooner or later scientists will have all the data they need to understand every aspect of human behaviour, and they can use it to design incentives that guarantee we respond correctly. The reward: consistency and certainty.

There are massive problems with this vision, not least of which is that the seedbed for many experiments in social efficiency (using social influence to drive behaviour) has been Facebook – which is not what anyone would describe as an unambiguously successful social experiment.

The physics of Pentland's social physics seems overwhelmingly Newtonian: a basic model in which simple causes provoke predictable effects. But from a quantum perspective, one that deals with large numbers and distributions, while uncertainty might reduce across millions of people, it is implausible to expect to eliminate uncertainty at the individual level. Predictability only exists at scale, which flattens out large variabilities, but that doesn't work if it's just you or me. Ideas and behaviours may be contagious but some people will always be immune; what's to be done with them?

The mechanistic vision also assumes that machines don't make mistakes, a faith few software developers endorse. Machines might not tire easily, but just because they aren't human doesn't guarantee they are infallible, a lesson made tragically clear by the proliferation of cybercrime, computer and airline crashes and the Post Office's Horizon software scandal, in which hundreds of postmasters were prosecuted for theft, which turned out to have been down to faulty technology. One of the greatest miscarriages of justice in British legal history – a computer glitch.

As even AI scientists concede, data can often be ambiguous and subject to interpretation, never more so than when assigning causality. Moreover, experimental data on human behaviour has proved notoriously difficult to replicate – perhaps because we humans aren't such standardized units after all.[11]

Pentland's scenario neatly sidesteps questions of who decides what constitutes good behaviour – and who decides who decides. It proposes entire societies governed by a single overarching system and homogenous mindset, the very definition of fragility.

Those reservations, however, didn't stop policy makers from swooning at the prospect of such perfection. In 2020, Sidewalk Labs, a subsidiary of Alphabet (Google), pitched and won the opportunity to work with the city of Toronto developing 12 acres along the city's waterfront. The vision was, in essence, the apotheosis of Pentland's dream: a dome-covered frictionless world where everything ran perfectly, thanks to sensors and technology that could 'unlock' services for residents. The more data you contributed, the greater access you got to robo-taxis, certain stores or preferential interest rates. 'Constantly thinking three steps ahead about what could go wrong and nudging us collectively', the digitized ecosystem used your 'digital reputation data' to generate rewards for good behaviour. Each morning you woke and looked at yourself in the mirror, hidden sensors analysed your stress and blood oxygen levels, all part of a massive, centralized data collection system predicting people's movements, controlling public services and law enforcement.[12] All it required was that everyone buy in and nothing go wrong, ever. No glitches. No hackers. No surprises.[13]

At first this ambitious thought experiment attracted powerful friends like Justin Trudeau, eager to bring investment to Toronto and to demonstrate his technology chops. That companies and governments serve different masters – public companies their shareholders and governments their citizens – was just one issue. Privacy was another. Slowly and painfully, Torontonians gleaned the morass of ethical and philosophical concerns that lay behind the project's glitzy marketing. Google/Sidewalk's promotional efforts looked oddly similar to political campaigns, complete with opposition research and attempts to co-opt privacy advocates. The company's public meetings were described as a masterclass in 'arrogance and gaslighting', while Jim Balsillie, former co-CEO of Blackberry, a man who understood technology and data, highlighted the plan's 'major implications for privacy, prosperity, freedom and democracy.'[14] As a combination of local activists and legal challenges unpicked the details of exactly what this daydream would mean to civic society and personal freedoms, its allure tarnished, and Sidewalk skulked out of town.

But what remains is an important legacy: a more-than-thought experiment that beautifully illustrates the high price that has to be paid for certainty. Not just financial cost (which made Google quit), but the human cost: in freedom, imagination, privacy, agency, even identity – at what point does being treated like a robot turn you into one? Seen in this context, the biggest threat that uncertainty poses isn't the discomfort of not knowing, but that our terror drives us to pursue certainty at any price. Beyond freedom and dignity indeed.

That it got so far reveals just how far we might be prepared to go, the sacrifices we might be tempted to make, to avoid uncertainty. But this implicit binary choice – between digital enslavement or analogue chaos – is a false one. The world is full of people who don't deny but who thrive by embracing uncertainty. They tend to be more optimistic, seeing uncertainty not as a threat but as an opportunity, a moment in time *before* choices are foreclosed. Not knowing what could happen isn't a flaw but a feature – uncertainty the great propulsive power behind curiosity, learning, discovery and invention, the essence of being human.

'We are never sure of anything', the physicist Carlo Rovelli says of his fellow scientists.[15] Not knowing is what drives them to explore. The true nature of science, he says, is its radical awareness of our vast ignorance. That there is more, always more to challenge and to understand is the motivating force behind his work. It doesn't numb, pacify or terrify him; it's exciting and enlightening. We may not know everything, but we can always discover and invent. The goal isn't an absolute state of certainty, but the continuing process of learning and imagination.

Rovelli doesn't buy the idea that there is an ultimate, final truth at the bottom of everything; he thinks this is a bad idea. Science keeps learning, which reveals more yet to learn; the process never ends. 'A forest seen from a distance is real. Get closer, it's real. See the atoms in the trunks; it's real', he says. The reality of the universe and of human life isn't static for Rovelli because there's always more to learn – and that's because life keeps changing.

Learning one new truth doesn't automatically cancel the old one. Such binary thinking militates against learning and there is good evidence that resisting binaries leads to better insights and decision making.[16] 'Reality is the ensemble of all these things', he argues. 'We understand reality by looking at the reality *between* things.' Once you reject simple binaries in favour of the true complexity of life, reality is no longer a question of whether the men in the caves or the shadows on the walls are real. Both are real. Both stand in relationship to one another. To reject uncertainty would be to accept the end of inquiry. To reject uncertainty would be to turn one's back on what is true.

Most famous for his loop quantum gravity theory, Rovelli can't be sure whether he is right or wrong, and he may not find out in his lifetime. 'The search for knowledge', he insists, 'is not nourished by certainty: it is nourished by a radical absence of certainty'.[17] While politicians may talk about 'The Science' as if it were a solid bedrock of certainty, scientists themselves acknowledge that science is only the best we know ... *so far*. The same might be said for all disciplines: history, poetry, astronomy, painting, geology. 'Between full ignorance and total certainty', Rovelli says, 'is a vast intermediate space where we conduct our lives.'[18]

Rovelli takes an intense interest in art. For all the rhetoric that imagines the two disciplines, arts and sciences, to be diametrically opposed, he sees them as sharing the same intermediate space: examining the relations between things. When he looks at an installation by Cornelia Parker, he isn't looking only at its individual pieces, but considering how they relate to each other, to him, and to his experience in the world. That's where the action is: in the interaction.[19] Novels, music and paintings don't aim to reduce our uncertainty but to provide richer means to discover, explore and challenge our experience of life. It isn't because we know exactly what the painting means that millions flock to see the *Mona Lisa*; it is the very ambiguity of the work that has captured human minds for centuries. Looking at it, I might reflect on when it was painted, how it compares to other kinds of portraiture, wonder whether the background is based on a real place, whether the portrait will always remain such a big draw, and why. Art can act as a portal to that liminal space whose pleasure is to see life afresh. Lacking even the practical rewards of science, we are drawn to art and to artists because it makes us think afresh and to feel alive. No art is an answer to uncertainty, but all art is a response to it.

On a less lofty level, it is *not* knowing that keeps us glued to detective, mystery and spy stories. It is also why audiences still flock to the plays of Samuel Beckett and Harold Pinter, whose plots revel in ambiguities that are never fully resolved but the experience of which is strangely and endlessly rewarding.

It isn't just that art itself is ambiguous, subject to interpretation, incapable of being nailed down. Whether Johannes Vermeer or Cornelia Parker, Henrik Ibsen or James Baldwin, Kendrick Lamar or Antonio Vivaldi, what is even more remarkable than the huge appetite to make and to enjoy art is the hugely uncertain lives that its creators lead. Almost every aspect of their lives is fragile, vulnerable to the vicissitudes of fashion, attention, luck. How to work, what to work on, assessing what's been made? What does it mean to me? Does it mean anything to anyone? These are the questions that suffuse every artist's career and to which there are no guaranteed answers. Poets, painters, storytellers, musicians, dancers, the designers of gardens and the architects of the built environment all grapple with *not* knowing every day. They start with nothing, mostly without being asked, and sail into the unknown with a passion to make something of who and where they are. That they can do it, and keep doing it, is a vivid demonstration of our capacity not just to tolerate uncertainty, but to flourish within it.

The popular conceit of an artist's life is one that is easy, even childlike, doing what they want all day long, with no practical concerns or hard decisions to make. The reality is that their work is crammed with hundreds, thousands of decisions, each burgeoning with uncertainty. Every word, every note, every colour is a choice that is also a hypothesis: I think this colour would relate well to this shape. That word has more heat in it, but will it keep people curious? The musical loops in this piece are fire – but are they overblown? As they answer the questions, uncertainty reduces, unless the decision is reconsidered and a new response found. And frequently, even when the work is ostensibly finished – the play opened, the painting hung, the music recorded – those questions may go on and on, pointing to what might be made next. With certainty, the artist could stop; with uncertainty, there is energy.

While all these questions reverberate, their plays still open on time, their TV shows fit into schedules and their films accommodate a million changes, demands and contingencies while still remaining coherent and convincing. Gerhard Richter's fear of chaos, he says, keeps him organized and methodical. The ultimate pragmatists, artists master new skills and techniques for no other reason than that the idea demands them. Their exhibitions are meticulously designed, the paintings and objects crated, packed, insured and shipped. Gigs and concerts integrate multiple media and technologies that (often to everyone's amazement) work compatibly and don't crash – and most of this is achieved against absurd deadlines and starved budgets. The working lives of artists daily defy the lazy cliché that to be creative is to be an impractical dreamer.

For critically acclaimed and popular artists, external validation might provide mental or practical security, but nothing can assure them of the meaning, importance or value of their work. They can't know what kind of experiences, feelings and ideas their work will stimulate in their audiences. In the desire to create something unique and original, they turn away from the predictable and reach out to what Toni Morrison calls their 'co-conspirators': the minds of others they don't know but in whom, as connection is made, the work of art springs to life. But who these people are and what the work means to them remains obscure. Even so, for the most part, they don't quit. Unfazed by what they don't know, they embrace uncertainty, setting off once again for new territory because it is in the search that they find themselves and the energy to see the world afresh.

Over several decades, I've worked with all kinds of artists: playwrights, poets, novelists, painters, designers, composers, actors and musicians. What I've learned is that the clichés and myths surrounding them could not be more wrong. These are the most disciplined, persistent and resilient people I've ever known. This doesn't mean that they are angels, of course; they've just the same foibles, flaws and weaknesses as the rest of us. But they don't choose their work because it's easy; they pursue it because it's hard. Driven by curiosity to make something no one has seen … yet. Accommodating bizarre exigencies and demands from a world that frequently marginalizes or ignores them, they persevere in pursuit of the new: new understanding, insight, disciplines and ideas. Serving the work, they rarely baulk when discovering what added mastery it will require.

In an age of uncertainty, it is just this capacity to join imagination with pragmatism, to start before the question is obvious, to explore and to discover that our polycrisis demands. New ways of thinking, doing and being are required if we are going to find ways to live that preserve our homes and our humanity. This is no binary struggle between art and science, imagination and data: we badly need both, and in full measure.

When we have so little idea of the skills, attitudes and changes the future will demand of us, the artist's open mindset is essential if we are to preserve the best of who we are.

However much we think about, monitor and analyse possible futures, we don't really know what it holds. Experts in forecasting now argue that the window for accurate predictions ranges somewhere between 400 days, if you're fantastically rigorous and practised, but just 150 days if you're not. They all concede that, even then, the unexpected will keep occurring. The one thing we can be sure of is that we will need to be very good at change, improvising and adapting to new and unforeseen circumstances. It is in these circumstances that artists have much to teach us about living with uncertainty.

Many institutions and companies already know this. It's why they frequently approach me, asking how to make their people more creative. They recognize that their old ways of living and working have become archaic: rigid, too slow, hard to change, slow to adapt and fundamentally anti-creative. Management was designed to reduce risk, but dealing with uncertainty requires taking more: to start before all the information is in (when it may be too late), to think beyond binaries, to imagine more deeply, to consider what's never been thought of before. A painting is not a solution to a problem, nor is a piece of music or a great novel. But the ability to think beyond boundaries, to develop ideas that are more than pat answers to recognized problems, is almost impossible to find in institutions today. But getting ahead of an unknown future demands imagination, creativity, the capacity to think freely and work across disciplines, and the ability and nerve to take action before it's obviously needed. That's what artists do all the time.

Yet for the bureaucracies and hierarchies that govern large organizations, this has become almost impossible. Working longer hours won't solve it. The whole rigmarole of performance management isn't delivering either. Precise job descriptions, key performance indicators, targets, goals and incentives work – they do make people do *exactly* as asked – but these actively militate *against* creativity, which requires risk taking, thinking about or doing what hasn't even been thought of yet. Giving people well-defined, straitened paths to follow makes the chances of them coming to work with bright new ideas vanishingly small. Throw in bonuses, precarity and surveillance technology, and conformity is guaranteed. So-called scientific management, a system designed for the certainty of control, is now a recipe for killing creativity, not engendering it.[20]

Nor do our education systems prepare young people for the future they face. Taught that for each question there is one answer, that identifying it marks them out as clever individuals who will get a chance of more of the same, produces good soldiers but is poor preparation for workplaces that now crave creative thinking, high levels of collaboration and a lifelong passion for learning and exploration. Our 21st-century problems are mostly now being addressed by 20th-century minds, the products of school systems that loathe risk, love rules and routine, and which concertedly defund, disparage and marginalize the arts. Lacking the skills that uncertainty requires, it's no wonder so many young people feel depressed, frustrated and afraid. It was said of Picasso that he had no use for menus; many today seem unable to think without them.

This is not just an institutional management problem. In the Western world dominated by an efficiency ethos, the overspill of management thinking into our personal lives exhorts us all to become concerted self-maximisers. Not just to quantify our lives (steps, sleep, weight, income, friends), but to develop the habits, modes of thought, communication and existence specified for 'a superior life product'.[21] The self-help movement has become Skinner's acolyte, keeping us on track, on schedule, walking, talking, writing in lockstep, looking more and more the same. We have freedom, we just don't know how to use it. Cleaving to rigid routines for work, health, family and holidays, we become more anxious and create yokes for ourselves in order to fit everything in. I am frequently reminded of the dancing bears of Bulgaria who, when liberated from a brutal working life into a wildlife refuge, still continue to dance.[22]

It doesn't have to be like this. We don't have to live like this. For as long as history records, human beings have been creative. Their creative energy went into making human life safer, healthier, easier. But much of it too went into works purely of the imagination. Pondering a definition of this art, archaeologists, historians and critics agreed that it was behaviour lacking any apparent practical purpose – but one that (according to that definition) goes back as far as 540,000 years, maybe even further.[23] This is who we are, who we have always been. Looking back at our history, it is human creative energy we most celebrate. Now is no time to lose it.

There is a great deal of mystique around artists, but the processes by which they see and make sense of the world could not be simpler or more human. While we might not all be artists, there is much that we can learn from them to enlarge, enliven and express our creative capacity, and to support it in others. Artists are frequently ahead of their time, gleaning through their engagement in the world the unconscious themes and needs that forge the future. It's why historians so frequently turn to the arts to identify just when and where change began. Sensors and signposts, they give us a handle on our times so that, instead of being bystanders, we can participate in and shape what comes next.

The artists in this book cover a broad range of styles and taste. Ranking is not the game here – they haven't been chosen according to any canon or metrics. Some I've worked with, many produce work I enjoy or admire. Famous, scarcely known, some still finding their way – all are thoughtful and pragmatic about their work, generous in sharing what they have learned, keen to be helpful. What was most striking to me, however, was that after every meeting, I left their company more alert, curious, energized and excited. It struck me that to make art requires, but also produces, an intrinsic optimism. What is the work for? Who knows, let's go find out. ...

The cost of certainty is high: loss of freedom, imagination, agency and autonomy, with no guarantees of human flourishing. While art alone won't solve all our problems, we stand no chance of addressing them without the open minds and disciplined courage that artists cultivate. If we don't want to surrender to Skinner's desiccated totalitarian daydream, or to my thought experiment, we will need the adaptive, creative, free minds of artists more than ever.

It's one thing to have freedom; it's another thing to know how to use it. And that's what artists develop. Eyes that are always watching, seeking, picking up on detail and anomalies. Curious minds that wander, drawn to ambiguity, asking questions. With courage and humility, they don't believe that anything is beneath or beyond interest. With the imagination to experiment, the freedom to think without banisters, the nerve to begin and the stamina to keep going and to change, their work shows them and us who and where we are. Who we might become and where we could go next. These are precisely the qualities that uncertainty demands of us now.

PARA ORCHESTRA

A disused warehouse in a grimy part of Bristol. Stepping indoors, my eyes adjust to the darkness and I take a Covid-19 test; the pandemic might be over, but with so many vulnerable players, you can't be too careful.

R&Ds are research and development sessions for devising performances. They're common now in theatre and dance, although much less so in classical music, where physical activity is mostly confined to seats. Today's R&D revolves around Mozart's 'Symphony No 40', one of the most familiar pieces in the world; you'd recognize it after the first three bars. But this orchestra wants to do something different: to demolish the moat that traditionally divides musicians from their audience, and to demonstrate how the different parts of the music are handed from player to player. One way to do that might be through dance.

Twenty Paraorchestra musicians attempt the first movement while performing a Faroese chain dance. It's insanely difficult to combine the physical movements needed to play violin, oboe, double bass, viola and cello while standing to master dance steps. Soon everyone collapses with laughter when it's just too hard. 'That was', guffaws conductor Charles Hazlewood, 'a wonder to behold.' Time for a break.

Charles founded the orchestra when, after 40 years of conducting, he recognized he had hardly ever heard or seen a disabled musician. But he knew from his own daughter that musical talent and disability were fully compatible. Searching, he found players of startling excellence and ingenuity, up for anything. 'What I've learned' he said, 'is that this is a two-way street, that we had as much to learn from them as they from us. I've jammed and improvised all over the world, but try that with a classical orchestra – they sit on their hands, no one wants to start first, and that prickly pregnant pause goes on and on 'til all the oxygen has left the room. But in the first session with the Para, it took 15 seconds to kick off.'

The ability to create a team around them that Charles found in disabled musicians astounded and inspired him. 'Eliza has mobility issues and has to create a team of people to get her on the train. Victoria is blind and needs helpers too. They're both brilliant at connection. I had so much to learn. ...'

Bravery begat bravery. Having shattered one paradigm, the Paraorchestra's mission is now to reinvent the classical orchestra for the 21st century. For Charles, who conducted the Royal Concertgebouw, Danish National, Swedish Radio and many other orchestras around the world, this has meant sacrificing a global conducting career, which only heightens the uncertainty of an already risky venture. Who is the audience? If the existing parameters don't matter, what does? Just how far can they go? Will anyone care?

If the dance doesn't work, perhaps putting sections of the orchestra on rolling rostra might? Clusters of musicians – some in wheelchairs, some with carers – clamber aboard and play while being wheeled silently around the vast space. The sound is tremendous, coming from all sides, miraculously in sync. The smaller ensemble passages come out with dazzling clarity. With groups of players scattered around, you listen differently; no longer a static wall of sound, attention is spread out, and you start to see and feel how the sections of the music work together. Next, they try a dance again. Instead of steps, the musicians will simply wander, snaking throughout the space. The sound is luscious and the space resembles a Fellini scene.

Charles and the movement director, Kyla Goodey, thank everyone: 'We will see you at some point for more madness.' Charles has nuggets of things that work, and clarity about which roads to abandon. Last night many musicians couldn't sleep, anticipating today's work. This afternoon, it's bittersweet. Which ideas will stay, which will go? At the next R&D, who will be able to make it? Who will be busy? What will happen next? As the musicians drift off, nobody knows. A few weeks later, Charles learns that whatever the piece will become, it is now scheduled to be part of the Proms.

1

Deep hanging out

In people's eyes, in the swing, tramp and trudge;
in the bellow and the uproar; the carriages, motor
cars, omnibuses, vans, sandwich men shuffling and
swinging; brass bands; barrel organs; in the triumph
and the jingle and the strange high singing of some
aeroplane overhead was what she loved; life; London;
this moment of June.

Virginia Woolf[1]

What a list. What a mess! The walk that Mrs Dalloway takes to buy flowers for her party goes on, page after page, full of impressions: the past, the future, the now. In the rhythm of the language, the reader feels her striding along, her brain buzzing, noticing what's in front of her, then wandering to an old friendship, a doomed romance, then back again to the street as she remembers the smell of the house, remarks on the bright-red hands of the florist and takes in the scent of delphiniums, sweet peas, lilacs, carnations, roses, irises and earth. Her character is doing what Virginia Woolf did all her life: noticing, paying attention, each detail a prompt for an idea, a memory or daydream.

The walk has a destination but the attention lacks intention. Clarissa Dalloway is not looking *for* anything. She's just seeing, taking it all in, her mind like a streetsweeper, collecting everything in front of her. In a state of high alertness, apparently nothing escapes her, but this is not a forensic exercise. There is no goal, no predetermined need for all this information. That it is random does not mean it is unimportant. All those details are material, but for what remains to be discovered.

Woolf herself was a great walker, in the city and in the countryside. It's part of how she worked: noticing, noting, stocking up snapshots and thoughts for future reference or never to be used. But she had a quality of mind so frequently found in artists: alert, thoughtful about the details that can so easily bounce her into a memory of the past or conjecture about the future. She followed wherever her mind took her, without, as yet, a map or a plan.

Many artists are walkers. It is a form of thinking: letting the mind wander, following it to see what is out there and in here. This is relaxing. There's a vast neurological difference between the conscious focusing on task-driven, intentional work and the loose mind wandering that Woolf describes. At the very least, the first is exhausting, slowly depleting cognitive capacity, while the second is restorative. And in that replenished energy, we find ideas and rediscover our creativity.[2]

That there is value in the wandering mind is not because it shuts down; far from it. Scientists distinguish between hard and soft fascination. Watching TV, web surfing, the cut and thrust of social media provoke hard fascination – they are entertaining but demand sufficient cognitive effort to leave people feeling less alert and frequently drained. Soft fascination, by contrast, is less goal-directed, more spontaneous, and allows for reflection. And we spend a great deal of our lives this way: over half our brain's energy is spent on inner events. But evolution is efficient, so all that activity is not for nothing. You could consider it a form of preparation, stocking the mind with what it might need in the future.[3] Doing so appears to make people more patient, more thoughtful and more creative, and it is frequently what we experience when walking outdoors. That it also helps people sleep better isn't trivial either, as sleep and the ability to think are tightly coupled.[4]

In our economic self-maximizing times, the discovery by Stanford academics that walking could boost creative thinking by up to 60 per cent was so alluring that executives rushed to make their walking more efficient by combining it with work. For a while, the idea of walking meetings and treadmill desks became a fad: walk *and* work! But this is specifically to miss the point that, even without the science, artists have known for a long time – soft fascination requires having no goal in mind. It isn't frivolous or lazy to let your mind wander; it's how you discover what you did not know you were looking for. What memory might bubble up or what image, sound or smell might trigger an imaginative journey to … who can tell? Without constraints or agendas, attention is set free.

An artist's work starts with wandering, soaking up detail, the vans and miseries and sandwich board men that crowd into life. Here the artist is a sponge, absorbing sounds, images, moods and colours, from shapes and smells and textures, none of which, at first, is any more significant or dramatic than another. If there is a point, it is to be in the world and open to it, stocking up on memories and feelings for a use that, in that moment, doesn't exist yet. At first the work is aimless and open to accident; it has to be because there's no target, no subject yet. Noticing becomes a way of life.

Charles Dickens was an inveterate walker, frequently at night, when he suffered from insomnia. Reading his description of *Night Walks*, it's clear that London had become so familiar to him that he could find his way in the dark. But still he discovers fresh images and spaces – an empty theatre yet with a candlelit watchman, the Dry Rot men who lurk and lounge through the night without intelligible reason. Writing in the daytime, these images haunt him so that the connection between what he saw at night and writes in the daytime becomes so tight as to be indistinguishable.

Many writers have depended on this body and mind wandering to pick up the mood of the times, to sense where the world is and how it is changing. Samuel Beckett picked up the habit as a boy, walking the hills of Ireland with his father: 'we were never going anywhere, just on our way.'[5] Henrik Ibsen walked the streets of cities and the countryside in Germany, Austria and Italy, scanning the horizon and people's faces, acutely tuned into the pace at which they walked and talked. An inveterate earwigger, he didn't just tune into what the gossip was about but also to the words and cadence of their talk, discovering that people grew more verbose as the day wore on.

Knowing this state of being to be so fundamental to creative work, the novelist Caryl Phillips started to sense that it was far from the way most of his Yale writing students experienced the world – their entire education had propelled them to be efficient, organized and goal-oriented. So he tried to disrupt that mindset by instilling alternative habits. Hoping they could untether themselves from certainty, he encouraged them just to walk down the street, look, really see what was around them – and then write something about it. Educational processes, he said, process people, training them with promises of rewards and grades and a nice place at a good university.

'But if you're going to be creative,' he explained, 'if you're going to embrace a certain imaginative life, you have to deconstruct this idea that X hours yields Y amount of rewards and fame. You can work hard and be serious, but that won't necessarily produce something of meaning. It's a much more tenuous process. They have to have a chance to discover for themselves what their territory might be, find out what is bothering them, discover what they might have to say. It requires patience.'

But the students hesitated, discomfited by so ill-defined an exercise. It wasn't what they were used to. Thoroughly trained to be efficient and tactical, they found the task harder than Phillips had anticipated.

'Because I hadn't given them a specific task, an assignment, a certain number didn't know what to write. I hadn't given specific instructions, hadn't said: "Go talk to someone at a bus stop" or "Go into a shop and ask for something". I left the door open for them to make a decision. Which panicked some people. But it's all about uncoupling from uncertainty. Just go! Look. Feel. Think. What's needed at this moment? What are we missing? If you can't keep your eyes open and be absolutely unconcerned with reaching conclusions, but more concerned with questions, then you'll write a book nobody needs.'

For artists, this isn't a specialist exercise in curiosity; it's a way of being. So I wasn't surprised by what Phillips recounted about the last time we'd met.

'I got off the train and walked to the hotel. Initially I was concerned I might get lost, but then I found myself looking at those Georgian buildings, and now, a few months later, I'm still thinking about those buildings, the significance of those buildings. I didn't set out to look at them or have them lodge in my imagination, but one in particular had a plaque identifying it as Chatterton's School House and that encouraged me to look at Ackroyd's novel about Chatterton and remind me that I haven't seen Ackroyd for years so ... that's how the process goes. It starts as a prosaic task – get to the hotel – and then I end up a few weeks later thinking about Chatterton and how one represents an artist's life.'

He starts to laugh. 'It's not a good time-and-motion study, that's for sure! You have to trust that if it means something, you will land there. If it is for you, it will haunt you and keep coming back and you will find a way. I don't think there's anything difficult about ideas – if you are alert to the world with a beating heart, you will have ideas. It is the thing that keeps coming back, won't leave you alone that is, in the end, worthwhile going 15 rounds with. But you have to allow it to keep coming back. ...'

The capacity to be alert requires solitude, to follow your train of thought and interrogate it. Living this way demands being where you are: earbuds out, phone off, willing to risk getting lost, following the path your mind wants to take. The other day, walking in Southwark, hearing muffled voices behind me, I turned to see a young woman with her headphones on; what I had heard was the online meeting she was attending as she walked. She was being highly efficient – getting exercise and fresh air while working – but her chances of noticing anything around her were practically nil. Where was she? If in the meeting, not in Southwark; if not in the meeting, in Southwark? Trying to be in both places left her nowhere. Our brains don't multitask; we can think about just one thing at a time and the faster we toggle between one idea and another, the less likely it is we will remember either.

So the walking that looks simple is actually complex: it requires having the sense of agency to go and to explore for its own sake, undistracted, with sufficient confidence to keep an open mind. What's key to the process is that it starts with no predetermined goals. If you haven't decided what you're looking for yet, anything can be interesting. Colm Tóibín, himself a keen social observer, describes the process wonderfully when writing about Proust, saying that he is always 'noticing, registering, sifting evidence and studying what lay on the surface, seeing what people wished to reveal of themselves when they appeared in the social world. He was concerned with manners as a painter might be interested in shade or contrast, as a composer might be interested in melody.'[6] Noticing, for artists, is foundational, a habit of mind.

During the pandemic, walking became more precious than ever: a single hour not just for exercise and fresh air, but where, temporarily liberated, strangers might see and talk to one another, seizing a rare opportunity. Near a piece of urban waste ground close to her home in Glasgow, the poet Liz Lochhead was gathering dead dandelions that she hoped to paint before their delicate hairs flew away when she encountered a stranger collecting bluebells. Their accidental, ephemeral conversation provided the seed of her poem, 'Chimneysweepers', a meditation on flowers, possibility, decay, and her mother. But she hadn't gone looking for that conversation, she couldn't have anticipated the encounter that three years later would pull in John Keats, Robert Burns, Henry Reed and Shakespeare's *Cymbeline* before her poem was complete.

At first, the results of an attentive life are mostly messy. When I asked the visual artist, Katie Paterson, what she tuned into, her list was extensive: 'Nature. Telescopes. Observatories. Water. Iceland. ...' She started to laugh at the infinite range of possibilities. But even in this random list, predispositions emerged. Her list is sensual: full of textures, smell, light. Not surprisingly, these turn up as key characteristics of her work. The studio where Lubaina Himid works is replete with her gatherings: Staffordshire pottery, toy vans, glass jars, old mobile phones, an old mirror – along, she says, with the chatter of passers-by, the barking of the dog next door. All get attention.

For the TV writer Jed Mercurio, scanning the horizon is a daily routine, which may or may not produce something of value. TV series like *Line of Duty*, *The Bodyguard* and *Breathtaking* emerge from an accumulation of signals, a process he compared to scientists' faith that fortune favours the prepared mind.

'So that is part of my cognitive process as a writer,' he explained 'which might be called seeking inspiration. But it's actually just a cognitive process where I build time into my day, and ensure

I have the functioning bandwidth to see what's going on in the world. It's just a scan, like a motion sensor. I'm just kind of scanning the sky and hoping to see a signal.'

With a mind emptied of preconceptions or the need for a quick win, it's amazing how much there is to hear. From the radio producer Michael Heffernan I learned the trick, when outdoors, of listening for layers of sound. The traffic would always be obvious. But then there were doors. Birds. The clank of a letter box. A conversation coming up the road. Strange lulls. The harder and longer you listened, the more you heard. John Cage, the master of found sound, heard music all the time, everywhere. 'There is no such thing as silence', he said, and the piece for which he is most famous, '4'33"', demonstrated just that. Its 4 minutes and 33 seconds of silence concentrated his audience on all the sounds taking place inside the frame of its duration. At a recent Vermont performance – a musician sitting at a grand piano watching the seconds – the silence attuned listeners to a nearby thumping car stereo, a solitary bird, sounds they might otherwise never have noticed. So rich was their attentiveness that many were sorry when it ended. For Cage, all sounds were music.

'You have to be open', the visual artist Jeremy Deller told me. 'Especially if you're working the way that I'm working: I'm not a painter or sculptor or drawer. So I have to be open. I try to be receptive to people. You have to be a sponge. You store up memories and thoughts about society and maybe later they reveal themselves to you. …'

Deller is a conceptual, video and installation artist whose work ranges from a bouncy Stonehenge, a film about Depeche Mode's mythic following in Eastern Europe, to a reconstruction of the Battle of Orgreave, one of the most brutal confrontations between miners and the police during the 1984–85 miners' strike. Deller's body of work is concertedly eclectic, often funny, always thought-provoking and full of ideas. He won the Turner Prize in 2004 and represented Great Britain at the Venice Biennale in 2013. The breadth and depth of his work is exceptional, a mirror image perhaps of how broadly he's prepared to roam, to discover.

'If someone wants to meet me,' he told me, 'on the whole I'll try to meet them. I try to be receptive to people so I suppose that means you try to be receptive generally. I live on my wits in the way that I work. You have to not be dismissive because you never know where conversations or meetings will end. And so you really have to be always scanning the horizon and try to work out what's going on.'

To the young playwright, Alex Donnachie, this curiosity seems to come naturally. 'I've always been a storyteller because I was allowed to get bored. I never sit with headphones in on the train or the tube. I listen to people's conversations, earwigging. I have so many notes on my phone – I found a note I'd written when I was working at a pub nearby and I'd written a bit of dialogue for a play I want to write. I know the whole play! It was all there. I'd been at the bar bored out of my mind and it was 11 in the morning and I just let my mind wander. ...'

Maintaining such open alertness, the Irish poet Patrick Kavanagh said, requires 'sensitive courage and sensitive humility' – the humility to pay attention to the unknown and the marginal – a glimpse, a sound, a biscuit, a pencil – and the nerve to keep looking for it. To find anything original, he understood, required respecting the elusive and the trivial. The German painter Gerhard Richter found this when his attention was drawn to snapshots whose very banality provided interest and integrity in ways that glitzier, more polished pictures could not (see Figure 1). Why? What lay inside old newspaper photographs that wouldn't let Richter go? Underlying the process must be a patient confidence that whatever attracts notice will hold meaning – somewhere. Eventually.

The novelist Olga Tokarczuk describes herself as being like a magpie, having an 'eye that is always watching' for some trinket or discovery. 'Things fall into your lap by accident', she says. 'I came across the protagonist of The Books of Jacob quite unexpectedly – I found a pamphlet of his disciples' writings in an antiquarian bookstore.'[7]

Her novel Flights can be read as a constellation of stories about travel, across continents, time zones, mental and physical boundaries. It beautifully matches porous borders with a post-modern erosion of narrative, all the traditional handrails, pointers and clues gone. The book grew out of travelling alone; without company, her mind and body could roam freely without any compunction to organize or explain her thoughts. She takes a history of anatomy course in Amsterdam, visits waxwork museums, discovers the legend of Chopin's posthumous heart, roams among airports, beaches, operating theatres, churches, among the apparently sane and the clearly mad. The reader is left with a sense of Tokarczuk wandering the planet by foot, car, train, plane and boat, taking us with her across an open world. 'Barbarians', she says, 'don't travel. They simply go to destinations or conduct raids.'[8]

You don't have to travel to move. For Virginia Woolf, reading was another way of being in the world, an addiction, she says, but not an opiate: quite the opposite. Seeking to help her readers understand what a novelist does, she urged her readers to recall their own street wanderings. 'Recall, then, some event that has left a distinct impression on you – how at the corner of the street, perhaps, you passed two people talking. A tree shook; an electric light danced; the tone of the talk was comic, but also tragic; a whole vision, an entire conception, seemed contained in that moment.'[9] Woolf's biographer, Hermione Lee, argues that for Woolf reading is so deep an imaginative immersion as to be indistinguishable from physical experience: 'And somehow or other, the windows being open, and the book held so that it rested upon a background of escallonia hedges and distant blue, instead of being a book it seemed as if what I read was laid upon the landscape, not printed. ...'[10]

For the reader, as for the writer, the essence of experience, whether in life or in reading, begins with a curious mind. Although Woolf is often accused of being elitist, she was no snob when it came to reading. Read everything, she urges. Forget about authorities and don't let them tell you what to read, what to like, how to feel; doing so destroys the spirit of freedom, which is the whole point of reading: 'If you open your mind as widely as possible, then signs and hints of almost imperceptible fineness, from the twist and turn of the first sentences, will bring you into the presence of a human being unlike any other. Steep yourself in this. ...'[11]

It is not always easy. She struggles, reminding herself to stay open-minded, which requires being alert to her own biases, the habits of mind, which, because they are habits, may be stale, narrow, too familiar for insight. Guarding against relaxing into those is an intellectual but also a moral exercise, challenging us to inhabit perspectives and attitudes not our own. That it demands and expands imagination both preserves our independence of mind and acts as a bulwark against brittle polarization: 'The necessity of magnanimity & generosity, trying to see as much of other people as possible, & not oneself – almost a school for character. The bane of prejudice.'[12]

Habits, biases, prejudices won't reveal anything new; they're built on familiarity. So the artist's, and the reader's, curiosity is driven not just to find something new, but also to find meaning inside the familiar that isn't immediately obvious. Identifying fresh connections, using those parts of our brain that identify patterns, allows promiscuous but attentive minds to discern themes, trends across all their street sweepings. It's an intuitive form of sense making without which nothing new emerges.

'Clip-clippety-clip, out of the newspaper I clipped things', is how Margaret Atwood remembers the genesis of *The Handmaid's Tale*. Her lived experience met her reading life and started to discern a breadcrumb trail of small news stories around women's reproductive lives. Countries where abortion was being restricted or banned. Jeremiads about falling birth rates. An Associated Press article about a Catholic congregation in which women were referred to as 'handmaidens' – a term Atwood circled. At the same time, she was visiting places – Berlin, Poland – that had lived through authoritarian regimes. But where all this was leading wasn't, at first, obvious.[13]

Today those cuttings sit in boxes in the University of Toronto's archives, but once they were collected in files, waiting for Atwood to glean patterns and weave her narrative. Remembering so much material is impossible, which is one reason why most artists keep journals, notebooks, records of some kind. J.M.W. Turner's watercolour sketchbook of skies, dating from 1816 or 1817, is thought to have been made during travels around England at a time when the explosion of Mount Tambora made European travel too messy and dangerous (see Figure 2). Like Constable, Turner loved 'skying' and thought that the variety of skies to be found in England was one of the finest features of its climate. To the casual eye, his book of some 60 sketches can look pretty much alike, but it's in the exceptional attention to colour and light where the rich differences lie. So the books performed several functions: they documented, as aides-memoires, the scale and variety of nuance, but sketching also helped the painter develop the technique to be true to what he saw. Turner is, simultaneously, noticing, recording and reproducing. To what end? At the moment of drawing, Turner wasn't working towards specific assignments, and today it is next to impossible confidently to assign any sketch to a specific painting. What we can see now is that Turner's sketches trained his eye, developing the technical power to paint such tremendous skies that, as in *Raby Castle*, they become more dramatic than the landscape itself (see Figure 3).

For Anne Hardy, interest is possible anywhere. The floor of her East London studio is her sketch pad, currently covered in large and small circles of dark earth. She's recently back from a residency in Marfa, Texas, and around us lie coils of rusted wire, some filling out a human shape with jeans and a hoodie. A dry aquarium filled with sawdust stands atop a pedestal with what looks like an iron snake inside. From the ceilings are hung random metal chains; upstairs a lightbulb changes hue in response to weather reports. Something about the arrangement of each item suggests an inchoate intention, but what this will become isn't clear – not to me at all, not yet to Hardy. The maker of large installations for public spaces, she expects that what the objects might mean will depend on the possibilities of context and her response to it. She will find connections but knows that if a piece moves to another venue, it is bound to change. She is still ruminating over the West Texas landscape, what she saw, what she remembers and what she is now turning it into.

'What I want is to spend time with the works, let them grow, mutate, to let it be itself. A lot of these works now – life forms or creatures, semi-human figures – are inanimate but animate. It takes time to let things accumulate.' The idea that certainty will bring peace, she says, is absolutely not true; the uncertainty of the objects is what compels her attention. Her studio sits in a tiny lane ending in a large Travis Perkins warehouse. Heavy vans, delivering or restocking, clatter up and down all day, flattening beer and soft drink cans that litter the road – raw material that we might regard as an annoyance but in which Hardy gleaned the beginnings of intricate fishtails. Working largely with found objects, she's drawn to the 'pools and pockets' that most of us would ignore as trash, but not Hardy.

'For the British Art Show, I had this idea of drawing on wild spaces in the city: interstitial areas where things gather and people leave things. It made me think about the city like the sea, full of eddies and deposits. Depositing feeling too. About how in a city like London there are gaps that don't follow the same rules, and they have that energy of potential and possibility.'

On leaving her studio, what I saw was entirely different from what I'd seen on arrival. Nooks and crannies in parks and alleyways now held interest that previously I hadn't seen at all. Walking with her, I thought, must be a tremendous eye-opener.

'I think there's always a sketchbook happening', is how the musician Soweto Kinch talks about his work. An idea will occur to him, he will hear a bell or a car horn, a strange rhythm in a train, and he'll take notes, sing or record the sounds on his phone. 'And if one of those becomes an earworm, for some particular reason, like I can't stop singing it in my mind's ear, I'll develop it more. It might be music or it might be lyrics. I don't really know, only that I don't want to lose it.'

For writers such as W.H. Auden, Mark Twain, John Milton and Samuel Taylor Coleridge, the equivalent to the sketchbook or voice notes was the commonplace book, a space where writers entered occasional thoughts and extracts from their reading that they might want to retrieve. These are thought to have been invented by the philosopher John Locke, who began his books with a blank index that he filled with categories into which he assigned quotations. The idea caught on, and soon booksellers began to produce notebooks with prepared indices and sometimes even ready-made categories. A current version might be seen in the design of Leuchtturm1917 notebooks that come with numbered pages and a blank table of contents. Artists as different as furniture designer Gesa Hansen and writers Ulla Hahn and Norman Ohler use them to capture incomplete thoughts, forgotten ideas. It's the evidence of what Hannah Arendt defined as thinking: having a conversation with oneself.

Commonplace books were not diaries, because, while those with chronological entries might trace a form of personal development, they were not designed to record events or activities. Instead, they are more akin to catalogues of the imagination, chronicling where the mind has wandered and what it has gleaned. Coleridge compared his collection to 'flycatchers', a testament to just how random his thoughts could be. Averse to writing in her books, Woolf tried hard to organize her reading notebooks, with separate columns for page references and quotations – but even so, life kept creeping in. Behind her notes on *The Canterbury Tales*, she sketched a map of Mrs Dalloway's London walk; other notebooks feature drafts of what will later become stories and essays. As ever with Woolf, life and reading won't be separated; she's uncomfortable with categories.

Auden's commonplace book followed tradition and was organized by subject, describing it as 'a map of my planet'. Unsurprisingly for Auden, there are many categories for landscape – landscape, basalt; landscape, cultivated; landscape, fens; landscape, limestone; and so on – a supremely ordered collection of random encounters with writers and places. Put together by topic, entries often collide startlingly, as when, in the section on 'Solitude and loneliness', Arthur Schopenhauer, George Santayana, Robert Frost, Simone Weil, Martin Luther and Dag Hammarskjöld meet, ending with a contribution from an anonymous Japanese writer of haiku:

> Letting rip a fart
> It does not make you laugh
> When you live alone.

Creative collisions can be brutal.

The value of the categorization is twofold: it helps writers survey the landscape of an idea. Because a large element of creativity derives from the inadvertent collision of two previously disconnected images, thoughts or sounds, commonplace books can be one way to see them. But categories can also be, as artists are, practical; it's easier to find that half-remembered quote or idea later on. Others are often content to trust to memory, confident that what is valuable won't get lost but will lie dormant within them, poised to emerge when needed. And this demands immense patience.

At heart, artists relish the randomness that invades all our lives, frequently without notice or intent. They aren't afraid of it but show a great capacity to find – or create – something of value within it. The street artist Lucy McLauchlan recalls getting lost in Joshua Tree National Park in California. She'd set out with some friends to find a bar near their campsite and, confident that they knew where they were heading, no one had taken a phone. As night drew in, the group started to lose their bearings in the desert. 'We'll get there', they encouraged each other. What was remarkable, she said, was how keenly she tuned into all the sounds around her: a breeze blowing east, dry soil scuttling through scrubland, birds as they bedded down for the night. Everything seemed vibrant and alive. As the bar came into sight, she reflected on how much more she had heard because she had no phone and no path; she was wholly focused on the here, the now. An accidental discovery. Her conclusion: if you want to make the years go more slowly, do something different. There's richness in the unfamiliar.[14]

This is not how most of us live today. Because we crave certainty, the market has supplied us with all kinds of tools and toys to assuage our neediness. AI, algorithms and advertisers actively fight any temptation to wander, keeping us tightly confined to predetermined choices.[15] Just consider the meticulously researched city break, defined and selected for us by travel websites, personal profiles and advertising. The cheapest, quickest flight, the cool hotel, reservations for well-reviewed restaurants and guided tours of key attractions – uncertainty has been eliminated. With all insights borrowed from others and nailed down before even leaving home, the planning practically obviates the need to go! All highly efficient, of course, but leaving no danger of surprises, this is the opposite of travel whose reward derives from that febrile sense of alertness we feel the moment we set foot on new ground, when, like McLauchlan, we know we don't know where we are and everything seethes with interest. And what do we always remember best? The unexpected. The cafe we just stumbled upon. Spontaneous conversations with strangers. The museum that sheltered us from a surprise rain shower, with its marvellous bronze sculpture of a bruised boxer. Getting lost and suddenly noticing all the streets named after physicists.

A mind refreshed, restocked and capable of invention: these are the rewards of uncertainty.

It isn't only artists who appreciate or act on accidents and surprises. Most entrepreneurs and inventors know that no one ever had a great idea at a desk, that ideas come from being in the world, not hiding from it. When George de Mestral set out with his dog, he was looking for nothing more than a nice walk. But he was observant and curious, so he paid attention to the tiny hooks of the cocklebur plant that caught on both their coats. The tenacity with which they stuck impressed him: VELCRO®, eventually. The idea for Post-It® notes didn't grow out of a strategic initiative but from wanting to mark pages in a hymnal when singing in a choir. Jack Dorsey's idea for Square (which began as a peripheral device that converted an iPhone into a credit card reader) came when he visited a friend selling glass sculptures at a craft fair – the larger pieces went unsold because the artist could take only cash. What I take from such stories is that while not all of us might be artists, we have in us the capacity to think like artists: making time to sense where we are, to leave the comfortable surroundings of our neighbourhood, to pay attention and explore with an open mind.

Even economists can appreciate the innate value of this. Chief economist and executive director of monetary analysis and statistics at the Bank of England, Andy Haldane was famous (or infamous) for what he describes as 'deep hanging out'. The term derives from the anthropologist Clifford James who argued for the importance of what Haldane did: spending time informally among ordinary people in mundane environments to sense what was going on in the world.[16]

'I did make a point of spending as much time outside Threadneedle Street as I could', Haldane told me. 'And it was wandering around or deep hanging out, with as broad and diverse a group as possible. Faith groups. Charities. Community groups. Trying to fuse it together, to make sense of what I saw and heard.'

Deep hanging out is what artists do, when they're wandering along streets, inside books, antennae alert. For Haldane, it proved a valuable counterweight to the language of numbers.

'I found myself relying more on stories than statistics, because the ways people behave (and some of the economic models that are towards the more rational end of the spectrum) have it that each individual is a super data processor, that we avail ourselves of information and probability calculus to make decisions about things. But we know that that isn't how most people make decisions. They use rules of thumb, heuristics. And sometimes the simple heuristics *are* better. So the best way I could find to understand the stories people were carrying around in their heads was to ask them to speak about what was on their minds.'

He paused for a moment, and then added, 'for a big introvert like me, it was a voyage into the unknown.'

Stepping off the predicted or predictable path feels dangerous to many people. They weren't trained to wander; it feels random and they don't see their peers doing it. But if you make the space for it, curiosity overcomes fear: what is over there? What does it mean? It's changed since yesterday – I wonder why?

Haldane worked for the Bank for 32 years and knew the danger of becoming cut off and institutionalized. So he didn't do all his roaming alone; he brought a multitude of different voices into the Bank. The danger, he said, was that the Bank was full of brilliant people – but all with the same mental models. So he brought in artists and activists with a wildly different experience of life. Tamara Rojo from the English National Ballet. Grayson Perry. Doreen Lawrence. Stephen Hough. Billy Bragg. People whose mental model was 'much more elongated'.

Challenged as to what he would say to these visitors, Haldane was frank: 'I would say I've no idea – that's why I'm doing it! I want to live with the uncertainty – that's the point. If I knew what Grayson Perry was going to say, he wouldn't need to come. And he didn't know himself – he'd just come straight off a plane from Japan!'

Haldane was also alert to the problem of power: that people are likely to tell you what they think you want to hear. But these speakers did not come in with a message for central bankers; that was precisely not the point. What Haldane and his colleagues cherished about the meetings were the wildly ranging discussions they provoked.

'Grayson talked about why it is that David Attenborough does what he does so brilliantly. Not because he has all the answers about nature! His genius is that he *doesn't* have all the answers and it's his curiosity that communicates such a sense of wonder about the world – and in some ways that is what imagination and uncertainty is about!'

'The Astronomer Royal, Martin Rees, alights on big questions and has the virtue of not knowing the answers. The excitement, the value is in the search for them. I think that is so powerful and so counter-cultural in our education systems, where it is all about knowledge over wisdom, or even over thinking. What is it Einstein said? Knowledge gets you from A to Z but wisdom takes you everywhere.'

Did he ever worry that his colleagues might feel this was all a bit niche? 'It's so *not* niche!' he laughed. 'We are cocooned in uncertainty right now – not knowing – and uncertainty is opportunity. It's saying the future is there to be created and moulded. Nothing could be more empowering – but you have to see how people who deal with it all the time, how they do that, what you can learn from it.'

Wildly popular, the talks provoked conversations that cascaded and rippled across the Bank for years. However dry and statistical central bankers might be thought, they were hungry for new ways of looking and thinking, and what they heard took them off the narrow lanes in which they had frequently felt stuck. That artists could derive so much from uncertainty changed how people thought – and how Haldane worked. He started to create more opportunities for deep hanging out: not just with external speakers, but in meetings without an agenda. With no predetermined plan any topic can emerge and conclusions come from anywhere.

'The skill I acquired in my final decade at the Bank was becoming a better listener. To process all those voices, it's a lot of work. It's so difficult, distilling what is in everyone else's heads. There are lots of voices, it's extraordinarily difficult, and sapping, and it does take practice.'

Deep hanging out is propelled by uncertainty. It doesn't go on forever because, over time, patterns start to emerge from the mess, suggesting a sense of direction, along with many dead ends. Much of that work is invisible and almost all artists describe a sense of their minds, their 'back brains', working on their collected material in ways they don't control. The musician and writer Kae

Tempest describes 'just following the idea. It leads the way and I follow and hang out with it.'

Neuroscience shows that what might look like bunking off is, in a relaxed mind, a highly active state. When listening to baroque music, volunteers' brains were most active during the silence between movements.[17] In repose, we use different parts of our brain, and it's then that we are most likely to identify connections and patterns. Sensing these refreshes curiosity – to follow what feels like a clue, or a trail. It's one reason why being bored can be so productive: because the emergence of an idea brings with it new energy. But for this to add up to anything requires that we put down phones, close calendars and make the cognitive and temporal space to do what might not look like work. That takes an investment of time and attention with no guaranteed return. It feels risky – because it is.

In the case of Henri Matisse, the wandering – geographically across a variety of landscapes, and artistically, across a variety of styles – tormented the first 15 years of his career. This was a desperate period, when he was scorned by naysayers as he struggled to locate the painter he felt himself to be.

'There were no painters in my family, there was no painter in my region', Matisse said later. Coming from a family of merchants, he was expected to join them or at least become a lawyer who could help the business. But he failed at everything he tried. Then, a fluke: bedridden with appendicitis, his mother offered a box of paints to relieve his pain and tedium. Now he knew what he would become. But his epiphanic certainty met only with hostility from a father and a community that regarded art as contemptible: 'When I said: "I want to be a painter", it was the equivalent of saying to the man: "Everything you do is pointless and leads nowhere"'.[18]

The fight that ensued was existential, each man fiercely defending his sense of self and meaning. Matisse was every bit as tough as his father and, with the support of his mother, eventually won begrudging agreement to study at the École des Beaux-Arts in Paris. For those 15 years he struggled, rejecting most of what his teachers wanted, meeting the requirements of the school only by the skin of his teeth. On occasion, he produced a work that garnered some small acceptance, but he refused to stick there and instead kept looking – and for what, he could not name, define or find. Travelling in search of light and colour, he would spend days, weeks from which he got nothing at all. Sometimes just a piece of pottery might hold a clue. Living on rice, in freezing rooms, with a stubbornness matched only by his infuriated and contemptuous father, he wandered among the possibilities of style, determined, as Rainer Maria Rilke recommended to young poets, to 'live the questions', but it was a brutal patience he needed. There was no guarantee he would be rewarded, only his father's certainty that his son was a lazy, profligate failure.

It can be hard (absent gifted biographers like Hilary Spurling) to imagine how excruciating this wandering must have been; Matisse had no reason to believe it would end well. He was no early prodigy, like Picasso, and the later sunny brilliance of his work gives little inkling of the fears that preceded it. His life embodied uncertainty and its challenge: a relentless drive to do, to make and to know, without any hint of a positive outcome. What we can learn from Matisse is not that there is some equivalence between suffering and success; there isn't. Rather that the invention or discovery of something original, creative, imaginative isn't a project starting with what we already know, can define and recognize – that would be a contradiction in terms. Instead, it requires inexhaustible curiosity, trusting to the experience of being alive. It's no surprise that the recurrent image in so many of his works is an open door.

For artists, the compulsion to make, a driving sense of agency, is fierce. Not having a project on the boil is itchy, unsettling. And ideas, gleaned connections, bring energy with them. But rush the nascent idea and it can fall apart; there aren't enough connections to make any sense yet or to point in any particular direction. So it's not surprising to find a correlation between creativity and a high tolerance of uncertainty. Waiting isn't comfortable. That tolerance can't be infinite – or the work would never get done. There's a period of suspense that any reader of detective stories will recognize. We have clues, hints. We think they must mean *something*. But what? Some kind of subliminal editing is going on, because quite a lot gets forgotten along the way.

Patience is tough when there are no promises or a hint of a successful ending, when there is no commission or contract, and no control over when the idea will emerge. Even for highly acclaimed artists, the next project could be the one that just won't come. It can still take years. Gerhard Richter had been thinking about Baader-Meinhof terrorism for a decade before he painted it. Why did it take so long? Richter isn't sure. He just knows that it often happens this way. He was interested but not ready – until, he said, something was open and he had to close it.

Waiting for an idea to force itself into consciousness takes courage and stamina. The novelist Sebastian Barry describes this waiting as 'very frightening and humiliating'. Uncertainty is intense; after all, what if the idea doesn't come? What if I'm not up to it? What if I wallow forever? Artists use a wide range of metaphors to describe the period between collecting and organizing insight – mulling, filtering, distilling, percolating – all processes that take time. But the filmmaker Mike Leigh has endured this liminal period often enough, and reaped sufficient rewards from it, to wait: 'I like being alone. Call it idleness, procrastination, gestation: these are all underestimated. You have to tolerate nothing happening, but nothing happening *is* something happening.'

Whenever he finishes a film, cast and crew are keen to find out what the next one will be about, eager to start again right away. But Leigh prefers long breaks between projects. This is a fertile phase for him: reading, walking, being away from films and in the world. He rejects the word 'zeitgeist' – it's too pompous or magical for him – but those interludes are when he retunes, refreshes his sense of where the world is. It's also when new attention can meet old memories.

'I was old enough to remember the time before the 1967 Abortion Act when people had unwanted pregnancies', he said, quickly adding that he was never responsible for one himself. 'For about 40 years I had this notion of making a film about that. But for so long, the time didn't seem quite right – and then, soon after 2000, it did, and that's when we made *Vera Drake*.'

The film won awards all over the world; why did he think that (as with so much of his work) it was just the film for that moment? 'I don't know why, why then. I don't really care. You can go to a garden centre and buy a ready-grown plant – plant and gloat over it – or you can plant seeds and wait for a long time while gradually, in an organic way, they grow. That's the analogy.'

Once again, neuroscience has shown what artists have always known: that our minds are busy when we look idle, that downtime isn't wasteful but productive. Lacking a defined intention isn't necessarily lazy. It makes us more flexible, better able to cope with uncertainty, socially more adroit and, because in reverie the brain mostly thinks about the future, more imaginative.[19]

But finding the organizing thought or theme can sometimes be focused with pragmatic questions: what resources do I have? How much time is there? What's the deadline? For Katie Paterson, considering what is physically possible in the space she is given can be a welcome constraint. For Anne Hardy, context is everything. Much may emerge through conversations with collaborators, producers, a triangulation between what the artist seeks and others feel and need. For others, the central idea comes after a long conversation with themselves, what Tracey Emin calls a 'system of thought' made up, primarily, of questions. It's not unlike our own experience reading a book, watching a film or listening to a piece of music for the first time.

At the opening night of Bristol's new performance space, the Beacon, everything was unfamiliar. The building's glassy spaciousness was exciting and fresh, but what the concert promised was obscure. 'Trip the Light Fantastic': the title implies fun, fantasy, but the mashup of Milton and popular music answers no questions. The concert hall was packed – 2,000 people – and the stage strewn with instruments, wiring and glass panels. The Paraorchestra comes onstage, all dressed in white. Music starts – but onstage, nobody is moving. Where is the music coming from? Look around: musicians, also in white, play while wandering through the audience, gradually gathering onstage. We start looking at each musician, seeking connections, clues, trying to make sense of what we are seeing and hearing. What kind of piece is this? Is that performer or instrument central to the piece? Who is carrying the tune? Where does it start? Writers, painters and filmmakers make much of our confusion, knowing just how compelling uncertainty can be.

A light show kicks off. It's hard to know where to look, even to know where so much music is coming from. Curiosity. There are drummers and percussionists, synthesizers, a full array of string players. Confusion. Charles Hazlewood's conducting is holding something together – but what is it? Intrigue. Patterns emerge as the two composers, Sinead McMillan and Oliver Vibrans, respond to one another with sequencers, samplers, loops and chord stabs. Two women leave, complaining it's too loud. (See Figures 4 and 5.)

Surrender. It's impossible to put it all together logically; better to give into the waves of sound and light, sensing in the audience rising levels of amazement and finally exhilaration: a celebration. The not-knowing keeps the audience gripped and leaves the concert in my head for months. Only much later does Hazlewood explain: the Beacon, like a phoenix, has risen from the ashes after years of disappointment and delay; the title is also a complex reference to Milton who was a ferocious champion of freedom of speech but also disabled by blindness. A standing ovation: that night even the conductor was amazed by what he saw and heard the orchestra create for the first time.

In Florian Henckel von Donnersmarck's film *Never Look Away*, at least an hour passes before we have any idea of what this film might – might – be about. Early on, we see a doctor, played by Sebastian Koch, but then he vanishes for an hour. We forget all about him as we follow the early life of an aspiring East German artist. At three hours, the length of the film allows von Donnersmarck to give us the experience that we have in life: moving past any number of people, places and things whose meaning we don't know unless or until the passage of time connects them. We wander from tragedy to happiness, from confusion, love, laughter and frustration, collecting and discarding memories, eager to know which will matter or what they will mean. That the film won't declare itself quickly is as deliberate as its length. Genre imposes a certain inevitability; the formal logic of an action movie reassures us from the start that, however disconnected a series of events might appear, the mystery will be solved by the end. That isn't von Donnersmarck's game. He is all about ambiguity and paradox, and that is what keeps us engrossed.

As the receivers of art, we look, read, watch or listen, confident that the details will add up, that meaning will emerge – because they have been shaped and curated for us. For the makers of art at the beginning of a project, no such guarantee exists. Waiting for clarity isn't for the fainthearted. The time requires self-reliance and optimism, the courage to look, the humility to see, the patience to wait. This makes the lives of artists unpredictable and precarious. But the capacity to tolerate equips them – and could equip us – better to function in a world that is similarly inchoate, confusing, befogged. In the end, the project won't be fully visible until thinking turns into action. Action is how we search.

PIERS PLOWRIGHT

Nobody becomes a radio drama producer because they want to be rich or famous. Many use it as a springboard to theatre or television, but the ones who stay appreciate a medium that is so cheap and quick there's always freedom to take risks, to try out crazy ideas, to fail and recover in a week. I never knew anyone to use that freedom with more creative genius and bravura than Piers Plowright.

I met him when I got a dreary job clearing copyright for material used in radio features. It took about a day a week, so Piers showed me a wall of commissioned programmes for which he had no producers. 'Take your pick', he said, so I did, making a show so weird that prize-awarding judges asked if it was true. It was original because I had no idea what I was doing.

But when you know exactly what will be in a programme before you start, it isn't worth making. The discoveries and surprises are what matter; they're where the life in a show comes from. In the four years that Piers and I worked side by side, he won the Prix Italia more frequently than seemed plausible, but he also made some real stinkers. I came to see that this was the point: not to seek security in repetition. He'd have hated the idea of 'Brand You'. His huge successes and failures grew from the same root. He wasn't in radio for fame or money – there was none – but for imaginative adventures, for himself, his actors and writers, and most of all, for his listeners. Do something different. Do it better. How? It was from him I learned that if at any point you thought of something that would enhance a programme, you had to do it, even if the show was due to go out that day. Not to do so was the only true failure.

He wasn't a saint. Writers who adored him were often hurt on discovering he loved others too. His curiosity drove him to encourage more artists than he had time for.

And his tastes kept changing, which was fun for him, but disappointing for creators who had finally found someone who understood them.

He was ambitious, not for himself, but for the power of sound. He rejoiced when a colleague in the department made a great programme, and I never knew anyone less interested in office politics. I used to think he was like a great 19th-century explorer, willing to go anywhere, try anything, to see what more he could get out of a sound wave or a radio studio. At work, it was clear – nothing else really mattered. My mother once asked me if I liked him. The question had never crossed my mind. I loved working with him.

He was my first real boss, and for years I imagined they were all like that. A lot of mumbo-jumbo has been written about managers and leaders (I'm responsible for some of it), but nobody has ever embodied the best with the verve and energy of Piers Plowright. That most people have never heard of him? Well, who cares? What they heard from him made its own claim to fame.

2

Into the forest

What I often do is plant seeds and certain things come
into fruition, and other things wither and die.

Steve McQueen[1]

Sooner or later, all that noticing has to add up to something.
But what? And when? Wallowing in ambiguity may hold
its fascination, but artists are driven to begin. Not all those
fragments will turn into a project immediately – Jeremy Deller
says he may hold an idea for 15 years before pursuing it – or never.
How the organizing idea emerges largely remains a mystery,
because so much of the process is unconscious, described always
by metaphor: a magnet inserted into a mess of iron filings. An
invisible editing process. Stewing. Mulling. The Japanese novelist
Haruki Murakami says he can sense physically when the moment
to begin approaches: 'After a while, the desire to write begins to
mount. I can feel my material building up within me, like spring
melt pressing against a dam.'[2]

Wandering minds are packed with observations and options;
one of them, or some combination, must claim precedence
over all the rest. At first, the choice can seem overwhelming
and fraught with difficulty: how is it possible to know which
path to take? None is guaranteed to lead to a fruitful space, so
all feel fraught with doubt and danger. The wrong choice could
waste time, effort, attention, and feel like failure. But the danger
of hovering, of not making a decision, is risky too: months,
years of wandering, and no arrival. Only experience provides the
confidence that one subject, theme, idea will overwhelm the rest,

but what, and when, and how easily feels random. Toni Morrison said that she only realized she had to become a writer when she went searching for a book, realized that it didn't exist, and knew she would have to write it herself. But not all projects announce themselves so clearly. Theatre director Ravi Jain recalls working on a project about climate refugees when he noticed a postcard referencing the *Bhagavad Gita.*

'I don't know what it was about it,' he said, 'there was something about that card, its image, but it led me to dig into the *Mahabharata.* I started to fall in love with it. And I started to daydream: wouldn't it be amazing if we could put the whole thing on stage in a day?'

The idea of staging one of the longest poems ever written was preposterously ambitious. Written some 4,000 years ago, its 200,000 verses tell an intricate tangle of stories about families, succession and a catastrophic war that ends the world. It is twice as long as the *Illiad* and the *Odyssey* combined. Indian children grow up with its myths and philosophies, which are central to Indian culture, but the poem is so vast that very few know all of its legends. To a Western mind, it seems both alien and familiar, with overtones of Greek tragedy, Ovid and Shakespeare. For Jain, that it had been staged once before, by Peter Brook, was both validation and a challenge. Brook's 1985 production remains a landmark in theatrical history: no one since had dared stand in its footprint. But it had recently become mired in a fierce debate around cultural appropriation. The name of Jain's ambitious Canadian theatre company is Why Not, and this time there were plenty of reasons why not. Too complex. Too expensive. Too long. It could never happen, so he went back to work.

Great ideas are tested by being ignored. If you disregard them and they go away, they can't have been that great after all, or the time might not be right. But those that keep coming back, knocking on the brain, demand attention. Artists know from experience that ideas are the easiest, cheapest part of the creative process: there's no risk just in having an idea – danger starts only when you act on it. Time, energy and attention are the artist's most fundamental resources; invest those in a project that goes nowhere and you will never get them back. Opportunity cost is real.

No amount of research offsets the risk. There's no data to be collected on future work – no five star approval from an algorithm promising success or failure – because, at the outset, the idea is inchoate. Nobody knows yet what it means, or could mean, what it contains or what it might become. The only thing to do is to start poking around, follow the idea and see where it leads. If to a dead end, you can only hope it's close by.

Once an idea has survived neglect or inattention, it operates like a searchlight, illuminating related ideas, images, sounds that were previously invisible. Psychologists call this priming: we find what we are looking for, however unconsciously. For Jed Mercurio, this second phase follows, and mustn't be confused with, his motion sensor scanning. Now he knows what to look for. The novelist Sebastian Barry says it puts the artist 'on a war footing': alert, sensitive to anything, even apparently useless things, that could now take the idea further. Noticing now acquires focus.

The great American documentary maker Frederick Wiseman began his film career with an insight from deep hanging out. Teaching law in Massachusetts, he became aware of the nearby Bridgewater State Hospital for the Criminally Insane. He took his students along to see a previously invisible aspect of the local justice system. And the place wouldn't leave him alone. He wallowed in it, absorbing a sense of the people and the institution, how it worked, gaining the trust of those who worked there. A film started in his mind. *Titicut Follies* was shot over 29 days, during which Wiseman filmed the bullying, abuse and force-feeding of inmates, the casual cruelty and neglect of the guards and doctors. Making his first film, Wiseman could have had little sense of how hard it would prove to get it shown or the opposition it would meet from Massachusetts legislators. But that first documentary revealed what became his lifelong obsession: the institutions that reveal American society.

'The selection of an institution', Wiseman says, 'is only an excuse to have a look at human behaviour in a wide variety of situations and to impose a form upon that experience. The overall goal is to do an impressionistic account of contemporary life through institutions that are common and have analogues in other places.'[3]

He has since made 48 films, all looking in depth at life in American organizations and systems: hospitals, modelling, the welfare system, libraries, intercontinental ballistic missiles, state legislatures, zoos, racetracks, the police. He follows no particular strategy in his choices – and he likes it that way. 'I have a running list of ideas in my head but it changes all the time because I have to be able to generate enthusiasm in myself and others. I like the idea of randomness, the roll of the dice. ... It seemed to me that a very appropriate institution to follow one for the criminally insane would be a high school.'

Wiseman's work and method have influenced documentary makers all over the world, including, in Britain, Roger Graef, Paul Watson and Kim Longinotto. All these filmmakers work patiently, waiting for the contours of character and narrative to emerge while filming without a specific plot or plan in mind. Commissioning editors, producers and administrators often find such open-endedness vague and inefficient; it scares them: 'How can you make (and why should we fund) a film you can't define from the outset? What guarantee can you provide that it will be interesting? What happens if I commission the film and it *isn't* great?'

But the absence of a predetermined agenda is fundamental to building trust with the project's participants and to the integrity of the finished work. When Graef began making a series of films for the BBC about Thames Valley Police, he didn't go into the project determined to change how the police dealt with rape victims. Had he approached his subject with a hidden agenda instead of an open mind, the people he worked with would have sensed his intent, felt distrusted and begun to distrust in return. The documentaries would have been (as quite a lot are now) predictable and, on a deep level, performative. Instead, Graef and his camera operator watched, waited and listened for what unfolded naturally in front of them. Patient. Careful. Paying attention. Because the story unravelled naturally in front of Graef and his crew, we felt it unravelling in front of us, too, so we believed what we saw. Our shock was as genuine as his. No filmmaker could have promised such an outcome from the outset.

Wiseman has always believed, he said, in paying 'as much attention to peripheral thoughts at the edge of my mind as to any formally logical approaches to the material.' He's comfortable with the uncertainty of where that attention will lead him because, by now, he knows that logic alone can only take him to obvious predetermined places, but instinct and curiosity will uncover what he doesn't already know. Watching his films, we get the benefit of his nerve and patience.

Here the poet Patrick Kavanagh draws a telling distinction between the provincial and the parochial artist. The provincial, he argued, 'has no mind of his own; he does not trust what his eyes see until he has heard what the metropolis – towards which his eyes are turned – has to say on any subject.'[4] Like the nervous commissioning editor, the provincial craves patterns, cares about fashion, longs to be on point. His mind is so full of preconceptions, editing and judging as he goes, that it is almost closed.

The parochial mind, however, digs deep and keeps digging, confident that the parish is universal. It is here, in a moment freely explored, that timelessness is found. Elena Ferrante's portrait of female friendship is a classic piece of parochial perspective: tracing in the dirty, poor streets of Naples the tensions of love and rivalry that transcend time and place. Jenny Erpenbeck always looks to the ephemeral and peripheral to show what it is like to live through history, her details more intense and intimate than her epic themes might suggest. Confidence in the value of the peripheral, seeing what others don't (or don't want to) see, also characterizes Jane and Louise Wilson's film installations, with the fundamental difference that they place their viewers right inside the contradictions they find. Their desire is not to achieve an ordered narrative; quite the opposite. Their multiple perspectives land us squarely inside paradoxes of power. You might say that they inherited that double perspective: they are twins who both studied art – one in Dundee and one in Newcastle – but whose work has always been made together. 'The conversation never stops', Jane says, 'even when we are three hundred miles apart.'

Rather as Wiseman spotted a subject at Bridgewater State Hospital, the Wilsons just happened to meet a man in Berlin while they were doing an artists' residency there in 1996. Although it was closed to the public, he showed them around the former offices and a prison that had been run by the Stasi.

'He began to find more keys,' Louise recalls.

'Then more keys and more keys. We were on the journey together, because even he had come in at the same point as us, really, like: "I don't know where this leads to!" So this was something that wasn't facilitated. We just gradually built up an understanding over a period of time. And I think that's been a strong form for how we've often approached things ever since.'

The exploration, which culminated in their installation *Stasi City* (1997), felt like pulling at a thread, but where it led the Wilsons didn't know.

'It starts to unravel as you begin to journey through it – but also in relation to each other, in relation to it. That became part of our practice, filming one another, looking through the space as well. So you're very conscious of viewing the site and viewing that recent history through the perspective of somebody else as well. It's very interesting to be surveilling someone who is also surveilling, because while we were filming we also had our guide who never left us. So we were constantly *being inside* the experience of the place.'

Stasi City became a series of rooms, each with huge screens conveying a sense of the epic, with images of the wrecked and abandoned offices, all entirely banal. Screens confronted each other with contradictory viewpoints, making it impossible to develop a stable, coherent narrative (see Figures 8 and 9). It's deliberately disorienting: one shot might lead down an eerie hallway; another leaves us static in front of a rising and falling lift. What we are watching is a restaging of places of interrogation that were designed to instil fear and anxiety. In the background, the sound of grinding machinery, a gunmetal smell and underneath, a profound sense of emptiness. It's impossible to see everything at once, to know exactly what is going on. At once alienating and compelling, because the images don't connect, the entire piece feels like a labyrinth, the exit unclear.

'It was quite haunting', Jane recalled. 'We used the prism of each other as protagonists in the situation so it also became an extraordinary conduit to being able to express that level of trauma. It was an extraordinary privilege to express what had happened there.' 'There was', Louise added, 'something very universal about it.'

All these artists began exploring without being asked. That's the acid test of agency: not just having ideas, but acting on them. This liminal period, between sensing and beginning, is sustained by curiosity – what could this be, become? Where might it take me? – and a desire to make ... something. A good idea won't be resisted. But it can fight back.

In 1980, when he was writer-in-residence at the Royal Shakespeare Company, Peter Flannery sat in on rehearsals of *Henry VI, Parts 1 and 2*. They prompted him to consider the epic yet personal scale of the plays. He started to imagine contemporary characters over an historic timespan, and his lifelong fascination with politics, police corruption and property development bubbled up. How does tumultuous social change test our friendships? How does our past play out in the present? In 1982, his stage play, *Our Friends in the North*, ran for just a week in Stratford-upon-Avon before it toured to Newcastle and then to London, where it was seen by BBC producer Michael Wearing, who wondered whether it might make a TV series. Wearing was a power in the land; he'd just made *Boys from the Blackstuff* (which had started as a single play too), and was about to make the landmark *Edge of Darkness*. Flannery couldn't be in better hands – and his stage play had shown him where to start.

Wearing initially wanted a four-part series that would end in 1979, the year that Margaret Thatcher was elected as prime minister. The original scripts included a Rhodesian plotline that was too difficult and too expensive; that got dropped. Fine. But then a change in executives meant the series didn't get produced, although Wearing continued to promise that it would, one day. The more Flannery worked on it, the more fascinating it became, until he had written six episodes, each set in the year of a general election. Flannery continued to research and write the series, avidly keeping an eye on police corruption in London, the miners' strike and politics in Newcastle. He felt that the series was getting stronger, that time was giving it ever-increasing texture, detail and insight. But his on-the-ground research got too close to reality and to government, and the Corporation took fright. One lawyer is said to have threatened to resign if the series was made, while others wondered if it could be set in a different country.

In 1992, scripts were commissioned. Flannery was constantly running into young script editors who read them and were eager to see it produced. 'When we are running the BBC', they would say, 'things like this will get made.' But their enthusiasm found no echo atop the Corporation. It was now 10 years since the original stage play, 10 years of uncertainty.

'I remember writing to Michael and saying "I don't want to ever ever talk about this again"', Flannery recalls. 'It was just doing my head in. It was always, always at the back of my mind.'

With the passage of time, the series had to keep changing shape because new final episodes had to be added. Flannery was writing on shifting sands. How could you rewrite characters without knowing where they were heading? How to pace the series when you were uncertain when it would finish? Flannery felt his scripts got richer and deeper, but with every year, the opportunity cost mounted.

'I'm vain, like anybody else, and I'm competitive like anyone else. And I'm looking at my peers like Alan Bleasdale and he's getting not just *Boys from the Blackstuff* but *GBH* made. His big hits were there! And I thought I'm wasting my life here. If this never gets made, I've just wasted my time. …'

But Flannery kept watching, listening, noticing, fine-tuning and rewriting. Uncertain. Daunted. Demoralized. Still fascinated and energized by the characters and stories he had set in motion. As time passed and episodes had to be added, the characters had to develop, deepen and change. And in 1995, the personalities in broadcasting changed too: the new controller of BBC Two, Michael Jackson, and a new enthusiastic producer, Charlie Pattinson, liked one another. Based on their mutual respect for each other's work, what were now eight episodes spanning the years 1964 to 1995 finally went into production.

'I still don't know to this day why Michael Jackson gave it the green light', Flannery recalls, laughing now. 'I know he didn't like it; he was very clear that he thought social realism was finished. And he looked at my thing and he just didn't get it. He used to say things like "Does it have to have the word 'North' in it?" and "Does it have to be about the Labour party?" I said, "Well what's wrong with that Michael?" And he said: "I just don't want losers on my channel."'

'It nearly broke me', Flannery says today. 'Only the loyalty of Michael Wearing kept me at it; he promised me he'd get it made. And he did.'

Flannery was never abandoned by his producers, but he was alone, with his scripts, with his ideas, with his characters. The imaginative capacity to keep in mind 160 speaking characters over a period of 31 years, the creative flexibility to reshape as the ending receded from view again and again, the ear to update the vernacular and the attention to notice the minute social shifts that distinguish one decade from another – all demonstrated the relentless energy, determination and curiosity that art and ambiguity demand.

It's no wonder that most artists construct around themselves a community of soulmates, a source of solidarity and resilience. To keep going requires others who know what it's like, who neither trivialize the fear nor exaggerate the chances of success or survival, who appreciate the emotional and psychological risks that are taken daily. That artists can be so open in their affectionate need for one another often leads to their being patronized as 'luvvies', slightly childlike creatures, soft and weak and not quite as tough as the rest of us. Nothing could be further from the truth; they are phenomenally and necessarily resilient. Willing to expose themselves to doubt, chance, condemnation – or to be entirely ignored. Fearing the work – but doing it anyway. Uncertainty isn't the obstacle; it's the draw. But to maintain such stamina can be a lot more fun, and a lot more bearable, in a group.

One of the earliest artist collectives, General Idea, grew out of the communes of the 1960s.[5] It came about accidentally when a group of conceptual artists wanted to mount an exhibition.

'We started acting out the figure of the artist – a parody of what was done in the art world just because it amused us terrifically. The idea of identity, questioning the whole idea of an individual, solo identity, was really in the air', A.A. Bronson told me.

Bronson, together with Jorge Zontal and Felix Partz (all pseudonyms), shared a house in Toronto and were deeply influenced by the example of Andy Warhol's Factory, when it was producing work in which Warhol himself was often uninvolved and which (at that time) he did not sign. They started to parody the celebritization of artists and the intersection of art, media, marketing and advertising, 'creating projects around the house that were collaborations without any framework or any name or any direction', Partz recalled. 'And I think at some point they just sort of smacked together where the working on each other's projects and the fooling around in the house became the same thing. And then, it became official.'

As a variety of different artists floated in and out of General Idea, all the work made together was presented under that name. All members of the collective used pseudonyms so that they could not become celebrities. Opposed to the idea of the tortured, lone genius, they were iconoclastic anti-heroes, producing their own media, first in print, then in radio and TV experiments. General Idea developed mail art, a postal system in which the messages themselves became artworks, enabling artists to connect, correspond and organize exhibitions. *FILE Magazine*, which acquired a global following, was an eye-catching glossy spoof of *LIFE* magazine's iconic covers, inside of which was a tabloid newspaper that allowed the mail art network to record their work and stay in contact (see Figure 6). Bronson, Zontal and Partz all did odd jobs, working in restaurants or architects offices, but also gained income from the Canadian government, magazine subscriptions and book sales.

The collective's one rule was to pursue only work that everyone, unanimously, wanted to do. Beyond that, anything was possible. They mocked the ubiquity and pomposity of brands with their faux TV beauty pageant (the Miss General Idea Pageant Grand Awards Ceremony), their own museum (the 1984 Miss General Idea Pavilion), a museum shop, an archive and even, in 1979, the destruction of the 1984 Miss General Idea Pavilion, complete with fire trucks, smoke and a helicopter. Multimedia experiments in networks included a live radio discussion programme conducted over open telephone lines (in 1972, deemed too difficult to broadcast) and an animated novella shown over a form of narrowband V (it took anything from 8 seconds to a few minutes to transmit a single image), proved to be harbingers of the future. A made-for-TV video series, *Test Tube*, included a talk show about art, a soap opera featuring an artist finding their way through the art world, and General Idea-produced commercials for cocktail recipes. When the Dutch national broadcaster refused to broadcast it – on the grounds that it looked more like real TV than art – the series represented Canada in the 1979 Venice Biennale instead. Over a period of 25 years, an efflorescence of experimental techniques and shows changed the landscape of performance and conceptual art around the world. It was, according to Bronson, a lot of work, but also a lot of fun, all the difference between playing alone and playing in a band.

The sheer inventiveness of the General Idea output is astonishing: its variety, humour and seriousness, the exacting care and beauty with which every piece was executed, the apparently unstoppable fountain of ideas. But there was a poignant irony in their invention of what General Idea had christened *Imagevirus* (see Figure 7). Their idea had grown out of the virality of art mail, where an image would be liberated from the controlling mind of the individual artist and spread around the world. General Idea's first *Imagevirus* appropriated Robert Indiana's pervasive LOVE logo, replacing its letters with 'AIDS'. In its brilliant red, blue and green lettering, the logo spread just as the disease did. General Idea turned it into wallpaper, installations, scarves, sculpture. It became public art, displayed in Times Square, on Amsterdam trams, on stamps, postcards and magazine covers. But this image virus now became more than a metaphor.

As Bronson told me, 'Once we knew that Jorge and Felix were sick, we worked very very hard. The work deepened and really started to flow. There had always been a social justice component to our work, it was part of what had brought us together. But it was always present in our philosophy and it was a big part of how we moved ahead. It was painful for me, of course, but not as painful as it was for them.'

In 1993, Partz and Zontal moved back to Toronto where Bronson looked after them until they died. At that point, General Idea ceased to exist. What's remarkable is that the inextinguishable creativity of this collective has continued to influence, provoke, inspire and infuriate generations of artists. For several years now, a major exhibition of General Idea's work has toured the world, tantalizing a new audience with their ebullient iconoclasm, beauty and wit, embroiling Bronson still in the work that he and his friends made for new audiences they would never know.

General Idea's influence can be seen across vast swathes of conceptual and performance art; it's hard to imagine contemporary art without them. And that impact continues. In the last decade, artist collectives have proliferated, testament to the supportive power of community and its capacity to make uncertainty so creative. In 2021, all five nominees for Britain's Turner Prize were artist collectives, in part because the pandemic had made an artist's life so lonely. Not all of today's collectives are as ego-effacing as General Idea, and while some, like Guerrilla Girls, promulgate a very specific point of view, others are just pragmatic collections of individuals pooling the means of production to make individual work. What sharing resources, whether of energy, materials, inspiration or moral support, can do is give artists more clout and endurance, sharing the wings. What they also do powerfully is cross-fertilize.

In 2005, Andrew Grant was running a young, small landscape architecture practice in Bath. He'd already accomplished a wide range of exotic projects – a palace in Doha, villa complexes for the royal family – but in the UK too much of his work seemed to focus on covering unsightly buildings or preserving what was already beautiful. He wasn't ambitious in a conventional sense, lusting after scale and fame, but he was hungry for more difficult, challenging work for his team. Then he got a call from the National Parks Board in Singapore. They were coming to the UK – could they meet with him?

'I had no idea who they were or what they were on about', Grant told me. An affable, relaxed man, we sat together in his discreet offices on the edge of the River Avon in Bath.

'Their government had sent a team to Europe, the US, Asia, just trying to get people interested in a garden idea they had. So we met with them; why not? They were lovely people. But to pitch an expression of interest, we had to pull together a team of architects, engineers, graphic designers. We'd no experience of doing anything quite like this – and really had no idea what it meant. None.'

At the competition stage, reluctant to invest huge amounts of time and money on projects that may never happen, many firms submit convenient, derivative ideas, based on work they've done before or seen elsewhere. But Grant liked the people they'd met and the ambiguity of the brief was a big part of its attraction. What excited the team was their sense that the Singaporeans wanted something truly original, a one-off, a project that would stand for something. So they came up with the organizing idea of an orchid.

'Orchids are the most cosmopolitan plant species in the world', Grant enthused. 'And Singapore had that aspiration to be a meeting place for the world. Orchids have incredible physiology – happy in harsh places, their leaves and roots draw in water even without soil. So they're a fantastic manifestation of intelligent design. And the flowers! Just the beauty, the diversity of flowers you can have …!'

Then one Friday night, the firm got a fax saying they had won the competition. The Singaporean client team returned and explained what they were in for.

'"We are going to build it," they said. "You need to start tomorrow. Refine the master plan." Our jaws dropped; the wholesale buy-in to what we'd proposed, and the fact that it was a multimillion-pound project when we'd never worked on anything of that scale before. …'

Like any artist, Grant was grateful for a client who brought faith, energy, ambition and funding. But in reality, nobody – either in Singapore or in Bath – fully understood what the Gardens by the Bay would become. They had concepts, brilliant ideas, but no one in the world had ever built a horticultural ecosystem of such diversity and invention. Biologists, electricians, architects, engineers, hydrologists – the cross-fertilization was immense. This was a commission of international importance, but whose momentum sprang from the quality and range of questions that now proliferated (see Figures 10 and 11).

Uncertainty hung over everything: how to create an environment supporting an enormous range of plant species that didn't harm but benefited the planet? Conservatories had to be a critical part of the project, but how could they be made carbon neutral while sustaining the plant collections? Where would all the water come from? How to deal with the humidity? How many people could be expected to visit, and how would the presence of crowds impact the atmosphere? Grant's idea of super-trees, 60 or 70 metres high, was thrilling, but would it work? Everyone yearned to make the site memorable, spectacular – but every new thought fertilized more questions, none answerable at the outset. Meanwhile Dr Tam, chief executive of the National Parks Board, had been brought out of retirement and was already on a shopping spree around the world buying up entire farms of plants: from China, Madagascar, Australia, India. ...

'Our diagrams started with the orchid, where the flowers were the gardens and the stems were the path network; that was the organizing principle. Everyone understood it as a way of getting into the project.' What Grant went on to describe was the organic emergence of obstacles and technical concerns, each one generating idea after idea.

Confident they could find ways through, every problem led to research that frequently pointed the way ahead, but also sparked even more ideas. The cycle seemed infinite. The team grew and, with botanists and lighting and sound designers and all kinds of new technologies and materials, they all had to learn at a phenomenal rate. Where artists fear repeating themselves, here they gloried in their challenges and renewed inventiveness. Using everything they'd ever known, they replenished their knowledge and understanding at pace. Exhilarating, yes. Exhausting, of course. 'But we kept pushing the boundaries and just kept going and going.' They started to conceive the entire park as a journey that reflected the excitement and beauty of their own experience, that sucked in new talents inspired by the ambition of an emerging vision.

'We realized we could give each tree its own ID and started working with a lighting designer from Japan who saw the possibility of using lights to let the trees talk to each other. And sound. From those early stages, it was clear that this would be amazing at night, to be inside this grove of extraordinary plants with a soundscape.'

Having started with a single organizing idea, the project propagated innovation. It was in the absence of certainty that all manner of new ideas became possible. What the team created, and continues to elaborate on to this day, went far beyond anything any of them had initially proposed. Ideas generated energy that galvanized action. That demanded enormous intellectual, imaginative and physical stamina. And mutual support: sharing the load.

In their first 10 years, the Gardens have achieved all the Singaporean team hoped – and more. A visual icon for the country, it became a destination visited by over 90 million people. It's easy today to look back to its creation as a dream, all the periods of difficulty, confusion, overwhelm and exhaustion forgotten, erased. But building as large and complex a structure as the Gardens also had to be pragmatic, full of designs and redesigns, ideas thrown away, resuscitated, abandoned. The team got good at 'killing their darlings', a phrase attributed to William Faulkner about the imperative to throw beautiful ideas out when they don't serve the whole. Because above all, what artists must do is keep going.

The biographer Victoria Glendinning observed that a large part of genius is energy. So, while the conventional image of the artist is often as someone who is lazy, somewhat infantilized because they are allowed to play around, the reality is exactly the opposite. Energy. Nerve. Daring. Discipline. When walking across ice, don't stop.

'Anybody who's ever painted a painting knows that it is a ludicrously difficult thing to do', according to the painter Lubaina Himid. 'You have this great idea and you think: I'll look at some other paintings – and that doesn't give you a clue because you don't see the back of the envelope, the layers of mistakes underneath. It is a fearful thing.'[6]

Matisse said he always felt a deep sense of foreboding before starting on a new work. Before she began a new picture, the African-American artist Faith Ringgold used to pray. No wonder Tracey Emin frequently sketches before attempting a painting; the sketch is a form of warm-up, giving her the energy and courage to start.

Even with creative confidence, the work is rarely plain sailing. When Haruki Murakami finished the first novel he attempted, he was disappointed it was so boring! So he tried a different approach: writing it in English and then translating it back into Japanese. Now he'd found a style that he liked. 'It felt', he says, 'as if the words were coming through my body instead of from my head.'[7] No artist fully knows what this piece of music, that painting, the next story will be before they start: it doesn't exist yet. So the rigour – not to accept second best – is fundamental to creating something new.

Fifteen novels and many short stories later, Murakami still never knows when the moment to begin will come, but when it does, everything else stops. He clears his desk and starts 'without hope and without despair', and he will keep writing every day until the first draft is finished. At the outset, he has no plan, no plot, no outline. He doesn't know where the story will go or how it will end. Like Andrew Grant, he is an explorer – curiosity drives him. Writing might be a sedentary activity, but Murakami is adamant that it requires stamina, so he runs or swims for an hour every day. He knows it increases the number of neurons in his hippocampus and thinks that makes his brain healthier, but he doesn't know whether or how it impacts his writing. That he runs a marathon every year provides an obvious metaphor for his work: he has to keep going for the long run.

When his first draft is finished, he knows it will be full of inconsistencies and contradictions. Sometimes, he says, he feels like he is sitting alone at the bottom of a well. No signposts. No maps. A complete rewrite will take a month or two. The book will keep changing. A third rewrite. Then a complete read through. Imagination, Murakami says, is the opposite of efficiency.

Writers as different as Lee Child and Olga Tokarczuk don't always know the plot of their books when they start. Curiosity is deeply motivating. Tokarczuk's novel, *Drive Your Plow Over the Bones of the Dead* is, on one level, a murder mystery. 'I became deeply immersed in the narrative', she said. 'I would wake up feeling impatient to find what would happen in the next chapter I was about to draft.' She had thought she knew who the murderer was – but later changed her mind. It was as much of a surprise to her as it now is to the reader.[8]

Lubaina Himid frequently works in acrylics, she says, because they dry quickly and it's easy, after she's had a cup of tea, to overpaint what she's just done. First brushstrokes aren't always right.

'There are lots of moments', she says, 'when it is a terrible painting and so the relationship with fear is about having to keep painting and dig it out of this terrible hole I've dug myself into. But I also use the paintings as a handbook, a manual, for how to be braver, so I feel the fear and do it anyway.'

Many writers, composers and painters love redrafting, although this may take years. George Saunders' short story, *Tenth of December*, took two years to complete. Don Paterson's poems read as though they were born fully formed, but they can be the product of 20 or 30 drafts. For Hannah Lowe, it may be 50. Jacob Sam-La Rose started one poem in 2009 that wasn't finished until 2019. While it is true that some works emerge fully formed – Robert Frost said that his most famous poem, 'Stopping by the Woods on a Snowy Evening', came to him complete on waking – it is more common for poems, stories, novels, paintings and music to result from a myriad of major or minute adjustments. Because each work is different, says poet Caroline Bird, rewriting isn't 'like fixing a car, where you can learn how to do it', or where the same fix works every time.[9] But having overcome the challenge of beginning, there is at least now something to respond to as the abstraction of the original idea yields to more pragmatic questions. The bifocal vision of enriched mind wandering comes into play: looking at the work close up and from a distance. Saunders learned how to do this while riding the bus to work.

'The time constraint handed me a finer microscope, which brought my attention down to the phrase level. I was almost exclusively micro-tweaking individual phrases to taste, not thinking about plot or story or theme. The decisions were playful and instinctive and even self-indulgent. Kind of like, I want it that way because I want it that way. And working obsessively on the phrase level started to produce plot. Once you had micro-specified the state of affairs by revising, it became clear what might want to happen next.'

When he refined parts he liked, and cut 'all the lazy shit' out of his story, the structure started to emerge around the 'good bits' that Saunders didn't want to lose. The questions became clearer: what gives or depletes a story's energy? How can you get to meaningful action faster? What Saunders understood was that you can't think your way to a book or to the solution for a book; theories of narrative or character won't help. Uncertainty is resolved by patience – and experimentation. Trying stuff.

After rejecting the impossible challenge of the *Mahabharata*, Ravi Jain was still trying to figure out his climate play when Why Not Theatre was invited to apply for a grant the size of which demanded epic scale. *Mahabharata* sprang back to mind, as if it had been lurking there, waiting to pounce. On learning they'd won, Jain's first response was panic: 'Give the money back. It's too big.' And his next response: 'Calm down. Breathe. Let's do it.'

But he was right: there were too many ideas, and Jain felt overwhelmed. What would his contribution be? The stories had been told and retold so many times, in song, in poetry, in dance. A 94-part TV series, *Mahabaharat*, made in the 1990s. Cartoon versions, graphic novels – *Sita Sings the Blues*. A Disney version, *Arjun: The Warrior Prince*. Comic book series in 42 editions; even a social media version in 2,700 tweets. Childhood memories, family oral traditions – and, of course, Peter Brook. What did Jain and his team bring? What would their unique contribution be?

He didn't know where to start, only that now, with money, he had to. None of the original problems – Brook, cultural appropriation – had gone away, but now they multiplied. Jain had trained at L'école Jacques Lecoq in France, where he learned to make theatre not by following a prepared script but by devising one with actors. This process requires a great deal of making and throwing away. Ideas are just proposals; they can come from anyone. What matters is that only the best idea wins. It's a radical, embodied form of writing and rewriting.

Jain believed that devising was the only process for finding the visual, physical, musical vocabulary to communicate the *Mahabharata* to audiences to whom all its concepts might be alien. But he worried that he wouldn't find enough South Asian actors in Canada with the right experience, so the project kicked off in London in 2017.

'It was great!' he remembers. 'We did a workshop. It was awesome. We really started chipping away at what it could be. We left with tons of ideas … and then it all started to crumble. It just got bigger and bigger and our producer just kept saying "yes" – to everything! And all of a sudden we found we had two creative teams, British actors, it was all ballooning spectacularly – and then #MeToo happened in Canada and that influenced everything. A lot of the organizations that we were part of started to fall apart. It was such a chaotic time. In March 2018, it all came to a head, and we thought the project would fall apart and I was lonely and depressed. I didn't know how I could get this ready for 2020.'

The *Mahabharata* was once described to Jain as a dense forest of stories that one needs to carve one's own path through. But where to start? Which trees needed trimming so others could enjoy the light? Would a straight or a winding route prove more rewarding? The ambition of the project, so much money to spend, the sheer number of stories and characters, themes and possibilities, everything that had made *Mahabharata* so compelling now became a torment. Jain got encouragement and moral support – keep going! – from the artistic director of the Shaw Festival, which had helped to fund the project. But he needed more than that – and he found it in Miriam Fernandes. Having both trained at L'école Jacques Lecoq, they shared an understanding of devised work: pulling at threads to see where they would lead.

Another workshop followed, this time in Canada. Unaccustomed to the process of devising, its ambiguity made the young actors anxious and uncomfortable. So they wanted to define their stories and characters too fast; they were used to solving problems, not exploring them. 'Because we were desperate and we needed something', Fernandes remembers, 'the work we made felt good. But it all became very sophisticated.'

Introducing two new characters – 'Ravi' as the narrator and 'Miriam' as a listener who kept challenging him – the team hoped both to contain the narrative and bring it up to date. In one central story, a war looms between two families, the Pandavas and the Kauravas. In a desperate attempt to win peace, Yudhishthira (a Pandava) gambles away his wife, Draupadi, in a game of dice. She becomes a slave of the Kauravas, who order her to be stripped in public. In the original poem, her clothes become endless – magic protects her. But in their new version, the character of Miriam challenged outright the misogyny of the story that Ravi told: 'I don't want to hear this story again, why are we telling these stories if nothing changes?' What they now call the #MeToo version of the story was indeed sophisticated – a story about a story – but now they realized that it created its own problem: it didn't put the audience inside the conflict, feeling what the Pandavas or the Kauravas felt. Instead, it left the audience watching from the outside, feeling smug.

After five years of effort, most commercial organizations would have thrown in the towel. But not these two. They recognized they were up against a hard problem that went to the heart of theatre: how to present stories that don't tell us what to feel or think, but that plunge us into conflicts where we feel and think for ourselves, to immerse us in ambiguity so that we learn how to deal with it. Instead of pre-empting the horror of Draupadi's disrobing, trust the audience to experience their own disquiet. 'We have to trust our imagination, and the audience's', Jain concluded. 'That's the deal: that they grow with us.'

For weeks Fernandes and Jain felt they were wrestling with the wind. Why not acknowledge defeat? Admit: it is just too hard. Jain had thought so the minute the idea had popped into his head. Maybe he was right after all.

But the great poem had got its claws into their brains. The stories weren't linear; the characters weren't easy villains and heroes. Everything pointed them away from binary solutions towards more wandering in the great forest where the poem begins. Something about the search was too compelling to quit. And anyway, when you're lost, finding a way out is a visceral impulse.

On resuming their search, they leaned more heavily on the poetry and brought young and old South Asian performers together, focusing less on big ideas and more on character, story, situation. More workshops. More writing. Finally, a script – a year's worth of work that ran for three hours. That felt, at last, like an achievement. But when they were asked if it was any good, they both knew it wasn't. It was now six years since that little postcard had triggered the idea for the project. It would be a rare luxury to stop and start again, but if only the best ideas could win, that's what they needed to do. Now they brought in more music, puppetry, dance, video, and just as they started to feel that they were getting somewhere, Covid-19 hit.

'Thank god for Covid!' Miriam says now. 'At the time, these things were terrible blows, but now we think of them as blessings. We kept writing. So much in the world was changing around us – and changing us too – and we had to reflect that somehow. If we wanted a contemporary take on the *Mahabharata*, it had to be part of the conversations we were having now.'

When an Indian dramaturg read their new script, his critique was rough but heartfelt. 'You guys have done a really good job of telling the whole story', he told them, 'but ... it's really boring! So linear, there's no point of view. All the characters sound the same! It offers nothing to the *Mahabharata* canon.'

Two new designers joined the team and their questions and reactions helped Jain and Fernandes to think visually and see the project afresh. Three themes, narrative pillars, emerged: the power and importance of storytelling was fundamental. So many of the stories were about taking care of nature that ecocide announced itself as a second pillar. The third was dharma: how we are to live together, the need for the strong to take care of the weak, for no one to have more than they need. These three eternal themes bristled with resonance. But after five years, throughout all of the dead ends, setbacks, criticism and confusion, what kept Jain and Fernandes going?

'Having a buddy', Jain said. 'There were points of despair; you get so you can't see which way is up, where to go, to dig or to climb. But the challenge of doing it and the exciting provocations: we grew as writers, as artists and thinkers, and it was something to chew on when there was nothing else to do.'

For Fernandes, the material itself forced them to persist, to keep exploring and find in themselves what they needed. 'It was', she said, 'big enough to hold what was happening in the world. Black Lives Matter was happening. Crazy forest fires. It felt like the world was ending. To be in that state and have the *Mahabharata* as the prism to focus through: it was a light in the darkness, an anchor. For so many artists, everything went away but we had great problems to engage with.'

By the time they finally got back into rehearsal, they had assembled actors of South Asian origin in Canada, many with immense skills in music and dance. Fernandes became the storyteller – not just on paper, but also on stage. This time they thought the script was nearly done, that it just needed some tweaks. But changing one piece set off a chain reaction, and now everything else looked different. A new actor in a role means all the other characters have to change. Decisions don't always end exploration; they propel it.

'It's not 'til you're watching it that you realize it isn't invention, it's discovery', Ravi said. 'Looking at what you've got in the room, the alchemy of the actors meeting each other and the music for the first time. That's when we started to understand that discovery comes from the inside out. For instance, when we discovered that Jay is such a great dancer, we cut the entire war and made it into a Shiva dance.'

The pair learned from the tortuous experience of making it what the *Mahabharata* had to teach them about uncertainty: the need to keep asking higher-order questions. With real momentum now, geography, gender, age, culture, class melted away as actors moved from one character to another, serving the stories through dance, song, language and silence. They stopped trying to tidy the story up. Consistency in characters no longer mattered, because human beings are inconsistent all the time. The non-linearity of the 4,000-year-old poem gave them freedom. As Jain and Fernandes wrestled to change the great poem into theatre, they also had to let the poem change them.

'We surrendered to the complexity of the stories: it is life. Life is that complicated and that messy', Jain reflected. 'We had to stop trying to force it into some conventional shape that it doesn't have. I had not to get reductive, not to simplify. I need to keep us all in that place of not knowing so that the audience can share an experience that *they* don't know what's going to happen either. They discover, we discover, because that *is* life.'

After eight years of work, the *Mahabharata* finally opened in March 2023 at the Shaw Festival in Niagara-on-the-Lake, Canada. The performance ran five hours long, and nobody had ever seen anything like it. Audiences and theatre makers around the world applauded its ambition, beauty and inventiveness, its compelling, imaginative, multifaceted storytelling. It had come to life after all. The stories were still sometimes confusing – who were all these characters, and which should we pay most attention to? Where did they go when their stories ceded to others' stories? What did the songs, the dances mean? But after the pandemic, audiences understood uncertainty better than ever, and the confusion in the stories wasn't weird, it was familiar. Confusion felt exactly like modern life, and the audience recognized and embraced all of the poem's unpredictability, surprise, delight and shock.

As Murakami said, imagination is the opposite of efficiency. Efficient ways of working depend on repetition: doing bigger, faster or more cheaply what has been done before. But it is counterproductive when trying to create or discover something fresh, that has never been done before. Efficiency was the gravitational pull that Jain and Fernandes had to resist when their young actors craved definition. Try to produce work too fast and what you're most likely to get is generic, comforting, because it arrives quickly and is familiar, but disappointing, because it's nothing new. As they chased the *Mahabharata* over the years, life kept intervening, changing what the team saw in the stories, changing, too, what they found in themselves. Time became a crucial ingredient in their work, just as it would in Flannery's *Our Friends in the North*, prompting deeper questions and richer replies. Resisting the comforting lure of the sure thing takes discipline, nerve and patience.

This is a wildly different way of being in the world than is typical of politicians, executives and managers. These days we call such people leaders, because they make decisions and head up organizations. But in fact they rarely lead. When artists wander and walk, they lead in the way that they explore the unknown. But in other domains, those who purport to lead mostly follow: second-guessing the market or polls, copying competitors, desperate for the certainty of validation and trapped in old thought patterns and frameworks left over from earlier times or marketing gurus. Where artists strive for originality, a corporate preference for the tried and tested is an illusory defence against uncertainty that constrains experimentation and discovery.

Demand for predictable, efficient outcomes strangles innovation. When attempting something new, most organizations demand proof that the plan will work – before it's begun. But, of course, if the proof existed, the innovation wouldn't *be* innovation. Incremental change is safer: a different colour, new packaging, a thinner biscuit – all designed to reduce risk rather than make something original. And bosses wonder why employees become disengaged.

In the charity sector and politics, it's become mandatory to cite theories of change: frameworks that purport to guarantee the success of new initiatives. Investors and donors crave signposts and maps – to a land not yet discovered! The problem with theories of change is that not one of them does what the best theories in science do, which is to predict with increasing accuracy. The theory of gravity has that capacity, but theories of change don't.[10] That's why we have to experiment, try different paths, improvise, throw out bad ideas to make space for better ones, explore with the drive, doubt and daring of the artist. But a craving for certainty leaves us stuck, paralysed in the forest. Absent the capacity for mutual support, imaginative stamina and self-critique, we make nothing new.

Why are artists so driven to experiment, when the risk is high and rewards so rare? Because they appreciate that there is no other way to find out: whether the idea works, how the picture will feel, what others will see in it. Andrew Grant could imagine but not know how dazzling his super-trees would be or why; he had to build them to find out. Experiments are also an exploration of self or selves, living the questions: how good am I? How far can we go together? It's exactly the same drive that entrepreneurs demonstrate. Asked why they take the risk of starting a new venture, the chief reason isn't fame or riches; it's to find out what they're made of, to grow, to discover what else they might find within themselves beyond what they already know.

For all its deep uncertainty, an artist's work frequently follows a common plot. It starts out as an abstract idea, purely imagined and therefore perfect. Set to work and all of its latent questions, problems and complexities crawl out of the woodwork and run amok, leaving trails of doubt and fear – was this really such a good idea? Maybe I've made a terrible mistake. Am I up to this? Have I missed the moment? Perhaps I'm not as good as I thought. … 'It might be', as Sebastian Barry says, 'a pile of malodorous nonsense. You just have to leave room for that possibility.'[11] All these doubts are proof that the artist is being stretched, is learning and developing. But in the moment of making, it can feel like the test of a lifetime.

It's become fashionable but it's facile to trivialize fear of failure, to suggest that because it is so ubiquitous, failure isn't painful, frightening or traumatic. Such glib confidence is usually heard from those who haven't taken big risks or who, now successful, have forgotten the pain. When it's your life and your identity that are at stake, the fear is visceral, the uncertainty profound. After a work is finished, it looks inevitable; the scar tissue left by a million tiny decisions, edits, deletions, overpainting and murdered darlings are now invisible. But during the making, and the remaking, the delays and doubts, nothing about the process offers the placid comfort of inevitability.

Energy. Nerve. Decisiveness. Daring. Discipline. Stamina. 'Talent is insignificant', James Baldwin said. 'I know a lot of talented ruins. Beyond talent lie all the usual words: discipline, love, luck, but, most of all, endurance.'[12]

GABRIELLA A. MOSES

'It's even more intimidating where you're like the gringa díregora and it's not your first tongue and you're worried about how you're coming across in terms of your eloquency.'

Everything about filmmaking is stressful: the story, actors, money, locations, schedule. Harder still when it's your first feature and you're directing in a foreign language. Gabriella Moses' mother came from the Dominican Republic, but Gabriella was born in New York and grew up speaking English. Only six years ago had she started learning Spanish.

But the chance was too good to pass up. She'd worked for seven years on her own shorts and feature projects when she was invited to discuss a script by a Venezuelan and Peruvian writing team, Marité Ugás and Mariana Rondon. Directing someone else's film hadn't been her plan, but she liked the themes – human trafficking, sex tourism, keeping families together. As it was set in the Dominican Republic, she was determined to do her interview in Spanish. Which is how she landed her first feature as a director, working with minors on difficult topics in a foreign country and a foreign language.

'It's like the minute people hear my accent, they think: "un gringo, tu tiene una sento gringo" ["I sense a gringo"]. But if I can rise to the occasion, I achieve this great thing; I get to confront my Dominican identity, my very prideful strange relationship with blood-meets language-meets heritage. I'm definitely up for challenge; being a woman, being an artist – it's all an incredibly risk-taking venture. If I drown, at least I tried. ...'

The hardest part was working on a script that she hadn't originated. Becoming more involved with the characters, she wanted to make changes.

'And my producer freaked out a bit. We were in prep already; on an indie film it's usually just a month, and decisions are being made, so if you're changing the script ... it's like a lot of barriers.'

'I give my producer so much credit; it's her second feature so she's living in fear too, she has a lot of investors on the line. I wanted to do right by her and the story and these real people's lives, because this is not some fantasy world we're creating. ... And I'm also thinking I'm going to miss the moment, but I want people to feel I'm listening to them; it's a huge internal conflict – you want to get along with people but you don't want to look back and say I really blew it. And I'm going into the backstory, why I think the writers explored male fragility this way and I don't think I'm saying it as eloquently as I would in English and I know we are running out of time and my assistant director says we can fit the scene in, because it's short and there's not much dialogue.'

'And the producer comes to the set and says, "Why are you shooting this scene I hate?" And then later she came up to me and she's like: "I went to the monitor and it's all so clear and I understood and I loved it." And it's for all those moments when you fight for something in your gut and your heart knows it's the right choice, but you also know you're going to fail sometime and ... that's why it's just crazy. ...'

When *Boca Chica* opens in the Dominican Republic, the premiere is, she says, 'on island time'. More people turn up than there are seats in the cinema, so the opening has to be delayed to open a second cinema. Afterwards, '... people came up to me and said "It's true, it's real, that's how it is here." And I was so afraid that people wouldn't feel seen or they'd feel it was exploitative, but they feel a lot the respect and the beauty of the island and these people's lives. ... And then when we presented at the Tribeca Film Festival and my lovely incredible screenwriters said, "You know, this is not the script we wrote. It is a better script." And I said it wasn't true – but that everything changes at every step.'

'An eye-catching, grounded, coming-of-age drama that thoughtfully depicts a determined young girl rising above toxic and traumatic circumstances in pursuit of a musically attuned, artistically fuelled future' is how Jose Rodriguez summarizes the film when it wins the Nora Ephron award.

'It was the one thing I hadn't imagined. ...'

3

Call and response

A tiny woman wielding huge paintbrushes and rollers stands on top of scaffolding as she sweeps the adjacent walls with big bold strokes of black or white paint. Passers-by often stop to stare, chatting among themselves. Approving nods, shaking heads. What is it going to be? Opposite, a man stands on his balcony, watching her.

Lucy McLauchlan is a street artist. She's used to working fast, because in the early days of street art – when it was called graffiti – speed was her only defence against being stopped or arrested. That changed during the time she worked with Banksy, and these days most of her work isn't surreptitious. Now she had been invited to a street art festival in Grottaglie, Italy. She didn't know much about the organizer Angelo Milano, how legal the work was, or anything about the community. But she told herself: 'I'd never have done all the things I've done if I hadn't taken leaps of faith.'

Milano started the festival because, he said, he lived in a place where there was nothing going on. That meant it was boring, but it also meant he could do whatever he wanted. He didn't ask for permission or funding; he just invited artists whose work he liked. 'I have always been very active and when you work from nothing you have much more freedom', he said. No wonder McLauchlan felt she'd met a fellow spirit.

Her first, huge painting covers the backs of three buildings that enclose an impromptu car park, a typical area of abandonment until she arrived. She had spent several days just wandering the town, taking in its atmosphere, personality and rhythm. Noticing: who lived here? When was the space busy, when empty? What kinds of people passed by, and what did it look like at night? Occasionally she gets sent photographs of a site in advance, but they never include the details that she cares about: not the wall but everything around it – a tree, a hedge where the homeless sleep, street lights. She loves working outdoors, she says, because there's so much more there than in any studio. A great noticer and wanderer, what she sees may operate as inspiration, constraint or both. Context is everything: 'When I'm at the site', she told me, 'my antennae are bristling. I don't plan, because the work is organic. I get the ideas while I'm doing it. I know by now that it will happen. I already have so many ideas and images in my head. ...'

Her scaffolding rises two or three stories high and the painting is huge: two giant birds meeting over a nest surrounded by eyes. For three days, she improvises; it might have been faster but for the extreme heat. All the time she paints, she is watched by an old man on his balcony. When she finishes, he insists she go down into his basement to see his work. It's not the kind of thing she'd normally do, but she's rewarded for her daring. She enters a cave, a treasure trove of ceramics glistening as the sun gets in. He is an artist too. Elsewhere she just decides to paint another wall that might be illegal: a huge bird, several stories high, alone in a field, its breast covered in swirling faces (see Figures 12–14).

Unlike the artists who work, rework, redraft for days, months, even years, McLauchlan's work is fast, spur of the moment. 'Spontaneity propels, intuition guides', she says. Not for her the eight years of work that the *Mahabharata* required, or the 16 years for *Our Friends in the North*. She relishes the unknown and its limitations because they are aspects of life. That she can improvise so fast is because she's highly experienced in the medium she has chosen, and also because she's calling on all the noticing she's ever done – the minutiae of life, art, nature that artists clock and lock away for future use. She may not plan but she's richly prepared with a well-stocked, even overflowing, mind that remains alive to the demands, accidents and contingencies of a moment. The work is physically demanding but she loves it for the freedom it gives her.

'After a while, I can't wait to start! It's a bit like a jigsaw, only without the box cover! I make some moves, they might not fit, so I try something else. It's the most empowering thing you can do: taking ownership of public space that far too often is monitored or has been privately sold off, security installed, to interrupt the public attempting to enjoy often "dead" space. And it's so much fun because you get to watch the world and people stop and talk to you, ask questions, and that can tell you something you haven't thought of.'

Even when a piece has been officially commissioned, she works quickly: in a matter of days, the work of years. She is not aiming for something that will last forever; quite the opposite. Her paintings are a response to where she is, a specific time and a place, and that's what makes them feel so alive. But her departure doesn't necessarily mean the mural is finished: 'During those three days, the man watching me came out at night and sprayed words interpreting my murals. I was so pleased, because I feel that everyone should be able to interpret it. Who knows, maybe he took ownership after I left. ...'

When the Irish poet Patrick Kavanagh talked about the artist's need for what he called 'sensitive courage and sensitive humility',[1] he might have been describing McLauchlan: her courage to respond to an invitation and to befriend the ceramicist in the basement, and her humility in acknowledging that ultimately her work belongs to the people who live with it. Courage and humility might seem unlikely bedfellows, but both are essential for artists, to explore beyond the obvious and predictable while paying attention to the marginal. A lifetime of ideas is the bedrock on which her work depends; those bristling antennae never switch off – who knows what they might pick up? She will return to Grottaglie the following summer with, as ever, no idea of what she will make. Not knowing keeps her alert, curious, hoping for the unexpected.

That McLauchlan's work depends on a lifetime of observations, catalysed by a spontaneous response to the present, is just one of the many paradoxes that characterize the working lives of artists. Instead of avoiding uncertainty, much of their resilience comes from developing a rich visual vocabulary with which to respond to it. A single way of working wouldn't afford them many options, but learning to live with contradictions does. Instead of seeking to plan and control, they cultivate a range of techniques and expertise with which open minds stand ready to address the unexpected.

The painter Frank Bowling says that his map paintings came as a surprise to him; following the shadows on a canvas revealed what looked like the outlines of countries, and he didn't want to waste the idea. He resisted critical interpretations that saw these works as political statements; to Bowling, they were simply experiments in colour. Paintings, he insisted, make their own history.

He grew more and more interested in chance and contingency, amping up the uncertainty in his work. As he spilled paint onto canvas that rested on a tilting board, the work seemed to take on a life of its own. These paintings acquired the open movement and freedom of the natural world (see Figure 15). Knowing about painting, he said, arrives with doing it. When, decades later, he went back to Guyana, where he'd been born, he discovered the palate that he had been using all along: in the crystalline haze, the east wind and the water rising up into the sky. It isn't that Bowling couldn't see what he was doing – of course he could. What he didn't know from the outset was the outcome. If he had, producing the work would have been a chore instead of an adventure, a new opportunity to see afresh.

'I've learned to wait for the surprises – and when the surprises come, to try and enjoy them because you don't know whether you're going to get them again. One day you pour the paint and it goes all wobbly and you can't control it. Then sometimes it's ahead of you, and you think of something and make a dash at it, and before you know it you've realized it. You don't know when you're going to get this kind of thing again.'[2]

The deliberate introduction of chance into an artist's work doesn't make technique redundant; it calls for more. In Corinna Belz's film *Gerhard Richter Painting*, we see the artist confidently wielding a large brush laden with a single primary red, swiftly covering a huge canvas with rough geometric shapes. It isn't destined to stay that way; over it Richter applies a 2-metre long squeegee laden with green. Later on, bits of red and blue will peep out from underneath as the surface becomes uneven. With each new layer, a different picture appears. Richter moves like a dancer, but the physical effort of wielding these enormous, heavy tools must be exhausting and the skill required to use them to effect is distinctive and well honed; the canvases quickly come to life. Sometimes working on two canvases at once, he attacks them from all angles with different sizes of squeegee. Shapes and textures emerge and disappear as he adds and subtracts layers of paint. He is working not according to a preconceived plan, but to a process that he uniquely understands and to which doubt is fundamental; each new layer requires a response.

Beauty is important to Richter, but it is always undefined, ambiguous. Art critics say that his work is both emotional and ice cold, a paradox one senses he likes. When we look at these pictures, we might discover one or the other in ourselves. We could find both. No wonder philosophers regard paradox as an indicator of something true.

It is said of Richter that he spends more time looking at, and thinking about, the paintings than he spends making them. He is both artist and judge. He is always very critical, changing his mind, uninterested in applause. At the end of a session, he stands back and assesses: 'Hard to say. They could be a bit better.' Like all artists, he has learned to develop a critical (some say too critical) eye.[3]

'You have to be like a butcher, know where you want to cut! But the hard thing, the important thing, is to remain impressionable.' Rut Blees Luxemburg is a photographer and teaches at the Royal College of Art: 'You don't want to close off experience and sensation too soon. You have to learn to read the image and to have ideas about it.'

She points to a student's picture pinned on her office wall and starts to describe all the puzzles and possibilities in it. 'A red floor. A green cloth. What is underneath the cloth? Maybe nothing. It's a puzzle, a riddle. Why is the backdrop torn? What does that mean? All those questions are why I look at it every day; I'm never bored. It's reassuring that someone noticed this; it means I'm not alone.' (See Figures 16 and 17.)

An element key to art teaching is 'the crit' when artists share their work with colleagues and gather their responses. It's important, Luxemburg says, to respond and try to take the thing apart – not to destruction, but to identify what artists themselves might not see in their own work. It's how they evolve judgement and originality.

'What's your intention? Why does it matter? It's not problem solving. Problems can be helpful. You don't want to explain everything – accidents can be very helpful too – but you want to find more ways of seeing your thoughts and developing them.'

A plethora of ideas, techniques, processes, an open mind and a critical eye – these are tremendously fertile methods for embracing uncertainty, propagating a wide variety of options. We may not all be artists, but we can learn from them the sources of resilience and response.

That pragmatic paradox – being prepared with a well-stocked mind while staying curious and open to anything different or unexpected – is one of the motive forces behind performance art where there is a setup but no script. It lay at the heart of Jeremy Deller's piece 'We're Here Because We're Here', which was commissioned to mark the 100th anniversary in 2016 of the Battle of the Somme. Watching newsreel of Remembrance Day ceremonies at the Cenotaph, Deller was dismayed by how staid, even mollifying, the ritual was. No emotion. Just heads of state, wearing the same old suits, placing the same old wreaths – it was a dead ceremony. So what kind of memorial could memorialize the true horror and sorrow of war? Whatever he was going to do, he didn't want a lump of stone or brass, inanimate and cold. The subject required more ambiguity, vulnerability. The poet Robert Lowell distinguished between work that he called 'cooked' – perfectly polished, smooth, finished – with art that is 'raw' – quivering, vulnerable, transient. Deller was searching for something raw.

In researching the Somme, Deller learned how frequently the bereaved felt that they had caught glimpses of their dead, on a bus or a through a shop window. He imagined how that might feel. The jolt. Hope. Grief. Could he bring that to life? Could he find a way to honour the dead by presenting all their complexity and contradictions?

Working with directors from the National and Birmingham Repertory Theatres, Deller recruited 1,600 people to act as First World War soldiers on the streets and in public places. For maximum impact, the nationwide flashmob had to be a surprise, so volunteers were recruited through small ads that said little more than 'Something interesting is going to happen, do you want to take part?' They had to be between the ages of 16 and 50, because that was the age of the soldiers killed on the first day of the Somme. And they had to be fit and healthy for an event that would last the whole day. Neither directors nor volunteers knew exactly what to expect. For them, this was exciting – an adventure.

All over the country, volunteers gathered to be fitted with uniforms, rehearse how to walk, carry their kit and mingle politely and safely with members of the public. They needed to be seen, but not to be pushy or aggressive, and Deller did not want them to speak. Where feasible, each would hand out cards with the age, rank and regiment of the specific soldier they represented – the same information that would be on their graves after they died that day, 100 years earlier. Printed on nice thick card, each was a memento, an important object to cherish. As July 1st approached, the 17 teams of volunteers grew more excited, but nobody knew exactly what to expect. Central to the idea was that neither the volunteers nor the public could be quite sure what was happening. Grief is like that.

'This was a large public experiment', Deller said. 'World War I soldiers plus the general public on July 1 equals a punch-up? An outpouring of grief? Whatever. ... In the lead-up, I lost control of it. I didn't know what was going to happen.' On the day, the volunteers spread out from transport hubs across 17 locations. Passers-by – amused, amazed, aghast – started taking photographs and posting them online.

'You lose control of the project through social media', Deller said, 'which was good. What I really wanted was for the ownership of the project to begin with me and go to the participants and then filter out to become the public. They were the ones it was for.'

Footage from the day shows surreal images of the past in the present: First World War soldiers at IKEA, on tube trains, in car parks and supermarkets looking like ghosts, hallucinations.[4] People are puzzled, uncertain, tearful. Some walk right on by. Many stop. Watch. Move on. It's a shocking, unforgettable scene: the war dead among us. For anyone who has ever lost anyone, a visceral reminder of what war does: 'We had to go to places that were awkward and maybe that's what art is, going to somewhere where you really are not sure what the reaction might be.'

By evening, it was all over. The soldiers stood in a circle singing the words 'We're here because we're here' to the tune of 'Auld Lang Syne', and that was it: a viral artwork that had spread through the body of the country. Deller had said he wanted the event to be ephemeral, leaving trace elements in people's memories and online, 'this 21st-century place'. The work of years, over in a day. Like quite a few of Deller's works, it's tight in its preparation, loose in its performance. Comfortable with uncertainty, it gains strength by adapting to what it meets. In that respect, it's a little like jazz – it's all about the response.

Improvisation in jazz has always drawn its energy and attraction from uncertainty: not quite knowing what will happen next. It is one of the many ways and reasons it stands in contrast to the Western classical music tradition where notes, structure, pace, volume and theme can be so clearly defined. Classical singers and instrumentalists might sometimes add incidental decoration, but the genius of Western music notation is that it is designed to nail down as tightly as possible exactly how composers want their work played. But when Miles Davis invited five musicians to collaborate on his album *Kind of Blue*, he wasn't after that kind of certainty. He wanted the opposite.

Nothing about the production of *Kind of Blue* augured well for one of the greatest jazz recordings of all time. Completed in just two sessions, working with Irving Townsend, a producer with whom he had never produced an album, Davis set the scene for an experiment. He had been thinking about the album for months, selecting the band with meticulous care – Bill Evans, John Coltrane, Cannonball Adderley, Paul Chambers, Jimmy Cobb, Wynton Kelly – were some of the great jazz musicians of their age. But the group wasn't harmonious – with each musician wanting to lead bands of their own, Bill Evans (the only white player) had already decided to leave.

On 2 March 1959, when the men arrived for the recording, they had had no rehearsal and would probably have expected to improvise from show tunes and familiar classics, focusing on shifting chord progressions that required soloists to move through a rich variety of scales. That wasn't what happened in these sessions. Miles was after a more stripped-down, modal approach, using only one or two scales, more intent on the details of a player's rhythmic phrasing, tone and texture. With the exception of Evans (who had composed one of the modes) no one in the band was used to working this way. Instead of building, as was typical at the time, crazier and crazier harmonic obstacle courses while also trying to create something beautiful, now each musician was expected to improvise freely but stay strictly within the sketch that Davis provided that day. 'If you put a musician in a place where he has to do something different from what he does all the time', he said, 'then he can do that – but he's got to think differently in order to do it. He has to use his imagination, be more creative, more innovative, he's got to take more risks.'[5]

In his autobiography, Davis said he wanted to move jazz on from its dependence on largely Western, European music theory, to open it up to Asian and African influences. He was after something alive, haphazard, that moved away from the musical platitudes he had grown to loathe. In the *Kind of Blue* sessions, he forced his musicians into a place where they had no choice but to play with complete originality.[6]

The recording starts with 'Freddie Freeloader' and kicks off with four pure notes, the 'head' played by Miles, backed by Wynton Kelly playing a very subtle piano with Jimmy Cobb on drums. Kelly's piano solo nods to Davis's melody, adding chords. Playing a long, mellow, melodic line Miles's solo is unlike anything he played before – or since. It's economical, it isn't bebop, and it isn't blues. It is something new and, in its call-and-response, it's definitely going somewhere. Coltrane, on saxophone, throws in a new idea, placing a mini note pattern in aggressive counterpoint against the 4/4 beat. More notes, more urgency, he explodes with ideas and lifts the pace. Cannonball Adderley's solo carries on that pace with energy; it's sassy and now it's fun. In the background, Kelly gently reprises the four opening notes. After nine minutes, Miles restates them again and the piece ends suspended on a soft dissonant chord. On the second take, Miles interrupts, telling Kelly he can't play a chord going into A flat. But on the third take, there are no interruptions, the piece is complete and in the can.

Kind of Blue consists of five songs, three of which were recorded in that first session. In the second session, on 9 April, 'Flamenco Sketches' was finished on the second complete take, and the trickiest track of all, 'All Blues', needed just one. When the recording was finished, Miles joked around, acting as though he was out of breath. There is no evidence that anyone thought they'd just created a masterpiece.

When people talk about why they love *Kind of Blue*, they enthuse about how alive it feels, there are 'things happening', it's 'a wide vista where anything can happen', 'a canvas you can paint on with your feelings'. The music seems to impart to its listeners the same sense of openness and possibility that the band had experienced on those two days: 'It gets under my skin, under my fingernails. ...'[7]

Kind of Blue is a landmark recording in music because it's the bestselling jazz album of all time, because it features great performances from legendary soloists, because it was one of the first times that modes were used extensively in jazz, because the recording itself is so clean and pure. All this required brilliant musicianship. But it also depended on intense, creative, critical listening – heightened alertness to what everyone else is bringing, while also imagining the best possible response. It requires absolute concentration in the moment while simultaneously deciding where to go next, living in two time zones at once.

What did it take? The improviser's paradox: both expertise and experiment are required to make the new out of the old. By challenging received fashion with an ancient notation, Davis revealed a fresh, new range of possibilities. This was intentional; Davis hadn't planned what everyone would play – he had prepared how they would work together. A third paradox: both a great soloist and a great composer of groups, Davis was 'a master at finding ways to make his musicians play over their heads'.[8] Embracing all those contradictions, where lesser artists might have sought to eliminate uncertainty, Davis counted on it.

• • •

How do artists know when a work is finished? Absent a deadline, they might keep working on a piece forever. Yet all the iconic images of finishing – breasting the ribbon, a standing ovation, the triumphant burst of the champagne cork – are belied by the artist's more prosaic experience. Olga Tokarczuk compares knowing a book is finished with the sense that she was hungry once and now can't eat another bite. At the conclusion of her 900-page novel *The Books of Jacob*, she treated herself to a cigarette from a packet she'd bought in anticipation: a strikingly downbeat celebration for eight years of hard labour, but 'a reward', she said, 'for the phantom theatre director, now that the curtain had fallen'.[9] Yet there's no applause, still no certainty.

An artist's work is made up of millions of tiny decisions taken one at a time: this note, that instrument, word, colour, shape. Each one forecloses possibilities for what can follow and uncertainty starts to shrink. This can be reassuring, because at last the work comes into focus, it becomes real. For some artists, like Gerhard Richter, that's a good moment. But it can also be dispiriting, when what started as an act of pure imagination loses the freedom to become anything else. Surrounded by containers of artworks that go back 50 years, the painter Anselm Kiefer doesn't think about art (any more than life) as a neatly managed project, defined by its deadline. Instead he sees his work as fluid, like a river that is always flowing, permanently in process. He sometimes puts his pictures out in the sun or the rain – and the pictures keep evolving as he leaves them there.

The poet Liz Lochhead cites Isaac Bashevis Singer on finishing: once you've gone through and removed all the commas only to put them all back in again, you know you're done. No choices left. But sometimes the work just won't leave an artist alone. William Faulkner's *The Sound and the Fury* started as a short story until he realized that it was too long and would have to be a novel. But telling his story through the eyes of a young girl didn't work. He tried again, this time telling the story from the brother's point of view. Then a different brother. Then with an omniscient narrator. None of these changes satisfied him. Even after the book was published, Faulkner could not leave his story alone. 'It's the book I feel tenderest toward', he said. 'I tried hard and would like to try again, though I'd probably fail again.'[10]

For Gustav Mahler, work on his 'Symphony No 1' went on for over 20 years, with each new performance followed by revisions that removed or replaced whole movements, or titles, or both. The piece's poor initial reception may have been one motivation but, in the changes Mahler made right up until the year before he died, crowd pleasing wasn't the driving force. It's as though he had set himself a question and the answer either kept eluding him – or it kept changing, as he did.[11] Context changes the work and keeps it alive, both for the artist and for the audience.

I asked Jane and Louise Wilson when one of their works was finished, and they hesitated for a moment, as though it was a question they'd never considered. Then they burst out laughing together, answering with a resounding chorus of 'Never!' Each time *Stasi City* is exhibited, that change of time, place and audience reveals different aspects of their work. When it was first exhibited in Germany, the installation exuded haunting impressions of the recent past, many of which lay right outside on the streets of Berlin. But when it was resurrected and moved to the Metropolitan Museum of Art in New York in 2018, it found an entirely different audience who themselves were now conscious of living in an age of surveillance; the subject was no longer history, but alive everywhere. How did we feel about it now? *Stasi City* keeps doing something that only art can do: it fuses the past, the present and the future.

'Almost instantly I want to go back and try it again', Soweto Kinch told me. A performer and composer, Kinch is best known as a jazz musician, although that description severely understates the range of his work. After he sends an album off for mastering, it won't be changed. But he's observed over the years that this moment of ending can be strangely exhilarating – not because it celebrates what's done, but because it reignites his enthusiasm to start all over again.

'I write some of my most exciting stuff the day or week after I've recorded a new album. But it's not like I'll go back and do that old one better. The next thing that I'm going to do, in some part of my subconscious, is going to be more refined, or different, or I'll get my point across better.'

For all that artists devote so much conscious and unconscious time thinking about the decisions that define their projects – this word, that colour, the right note – they are uneasy judges of their finished work. The crit develops their capacity to see choices and make that myriad of decisions, but what they now add up to, what the finished piece truly is, is hard to judge. Critics will make their assessments, of course, but what that means, how much it matters, changes constantly. Ambivalence on this topic was beautifully summarized by the cartoonist Jules Feiffer when he drew a playwright discussing reviews with a friend. Critics, the playwright recounts, had condemned his first play for being inept and drivel, but they had misunderstood it. Reviewers had likewise dismissed his second play as abhorrent and pretentious; again, they had misunderstood. His third play had been acclaimed a smash hit and a triumph; now they just misunderstood him to his advantage: 'In the arts', he concludes, 'that's known as success.'[12]

Try as they might, no artist can perch inside the minds of their readers, listeners or viewers to watch what's going on. But that is where the action is: *between* art and its audience. The one place where the artist is *not*, where they can't earwig or take notice, is in the minds of their audience.

'Fiction is as close as you can come neurologically to someone else's reality', Margaret Atwood says, because it's participatory. Like Toni Morrison, she hopes to enlist active 'co-conspirators' in a new way of seeing the world. For Lubaina Himid, it's when her work meets viewers that it really springs to life. She compares the meeting of those minds to that moment between a question – and a response: 'I've always thought of my work and my own conversations with it, as starting when people get to see it. It's how the past, present and future overlap and speak together.'[13] But there's no telling how that conversation will go. Yesterday's meeting of minds may be tomorrow's angry debate. And even that mutates over time, as life reinterprets what we remember.

That art speaks to its audience so intimately makes its reception inherently unpredictable, and few artists feel confident of their ability to forecast how their work will fare. Eight or nine months into the filming of *Our Friends in the North*, Daniel Craig asked Mark Strong, 'Do you think this is going to be any good?' Mark just shrugged; he had no idea.

When, after 14 years of abject uncertainty, *Our Friends in the North* finally went out, Peter Flannery was relieved just at it being broadcast. That it came to be regarded as one of the three greatest TV series ever made was unexpected from start to finish, even by the man who had dreamt it up. Repeated three times since its first outing, it continued to find new audiences who marvelled at their history, or their parents' history, at how much had changed – technology, hairstyles – and how much more had not: police violence, shabby buildings, local corruption, love and friendship, government abuse. Almost everyone involved in it had underestimated the work's power.

On completing his novel *Days Without End*, Sebastian Barry concluded that the book would sell poorly and that he would need to start another one fast. In fact, it made him the first author to win the Costa Prize twice. And whatever Faulkner may have felt, many readers love *The Sound and the Fury* just as he left it. But these happy endings are matched by at least as many, if not more, disappointed ones.

For a young playwright like Alex Donnachie, small failures carry a huge burden of meaning: 'is this a judgement of the work, or of me? Do I have what it takes? Should I give up?' After one of her plays did well at the Edinburgh Festival, she was invited to bring it to Prague, where a New York producer saw it and wondered about taking it to the United States. But in the meantime, she got a long-term role in a new production of *War Horse*. She appreciated the luxury of choices, but that didn't make them simpler. Should she stick with the sure thing, or take a leap of faith and go to Manhattan? These are questions every young artist will ask of teachers and friends, and no one knows the answer. Her passion for her stories and characters keeps her going, and she has found that surprises are as likely to be positive as negative. But combining sensitive antennae with a thick skin is a tough gig.

It's easy to talk breezily about the value of failure when it isn't your own, or when it's well in the past. But in that moment, a keen sense of public humiliation can be excruciating. When, after a string of hits, Peter Barnes's two huge plays in succession – *The Bewitched* and *Laughter!* – were panned with excoriating reviews, this most productive of playwrights couldn't write for months. Eventually he decided to start again from scratch, or, as he put it, to put his game back together, stroke by stroke, like a golfer. (It was a curious analogy – Barnes never played golf.)

He began with radio monologues, then dialogues, then trios: a deliberate act of renaissance. Leading actors now flocked to play his roles – Judi Dench, John Gielgud, Alec Guinness, Laurence Olivier, Ian McKellen. Seven years later, his play *Red Noses* took London theatre by storm: still recognizably his work, but different too – more complex, with fewer words and more meaning emerging between characters. His resilience had demanded but also generated a new process and technique. In not giving up, he had found something new in himself, but it would be trite to assume the experience had been anything less than traumatic.

That success in art is so unpredictable has come to seem, to many businesses, like a problem to be solved. This isn't new. The documentary maker Roger Graef's *Manifesto* decried the habit of commissioning editors to demand predictable success, arguing that 'predetermining a surprise is a contradiction in terms' and artists should be trusted, not nailed down.[14] But technology always rushes to displace the benefits of doubt with data. Much of the investment in streaming media has been driven by the giddy promise of watching the watchers. Early entrants like Netflix toyed with the possibility of being able to deduce algorithms that could guarantee hit shows. If data could identify which kinds of scenes, in what order, the kinds of characters and patterns of sex and/or violence that characterized the highest viewership, then mass-producing hits should be easy: not so much a Holy Grail as a Holy Narrative Template. That mission petered out when the resulting shows turned out to be monotonously the same, and sought-after writers and producers weren't thrilled by the prospect of making them. They all found uncertainty stimulating, inspirational. If a formula could promise success, why bother?

But chasing certainty is an easy trap to fall into. What excited a senior executive leading the introduction of the corporation's new Disney+ service was the prospect of data the company had never been able to obtain from cinema sales. At last, he enthused, executives would know exactly what kind of people were addicts, loyalists or casual viewers, imagining that the whole messy business of creating something new and untested would finally become predictable, cut and dried. When I countered that the data might not explain *why* people watched – did that show get good numbers because it was wonderful or because there was a paucity of better shows that month? Was it the famous actor or the rising star who captured the audience's loyalty? How many had actually stayed through the entire film, how many had slept through it, or had an initial audience of five dwindled to just one tired parent asleep on the sofa? – he looked, a colleague told me, like his head had exploded. Uncertainty was still alive and kicking. Even Amazon's Kindle, monitoring how much of a book we read and which sections we highlight, can't explain why we marked that section or why we unexpectedly stopped reading.

Jed Mercurio, creator of such monster TV hits as *Bodies*, *The Bodyguard* and *Line of Duty*, is more enthusiastic about data gathering, because, he says, it provides him with a useful defence against the unsubstantiated opinions of powerful decision makers. If influential executives just don't like one of his shows, the sheer volume of viewers who do can provide powerful counterarguments, making it harder for individual executives to have the sway they once did in Peter Flannery's time. And, as a former doctor, Mercurio sees both the value, but also the difficulty, of measurement and its interpretation.

'The difficulty with data isn't the data', Mercurio argues. 'The interpretation is the assignment of causation to the data and I know the limitations of those things. So this is Heisenberg's uncertainty: you change something by observing it. So if you ask people what they thought of a television program, you may be changing their opinion. Because they may not want to seem uncharitable. Or they may see this as their opportunity for a protest vote.' Huge data sets collected for TV shows can measure but not explain responses – and focus groups, Mercurio knows, are unreliable because the people in them influence one another.

For Lubaina Himid, 'the exciting and dangerous thing is that you can't predict how people will respond because it's entirely individual'.[15] Artists know and relish the fact that controlling the response to their work is impossible; the context in which a film or TV show appears, the day of a concert, the week of the play, the mood of the moment – they accept that they can never plan for the individual quirks and flukes of life. They remain genuinely curious to see what their audiences make of their work, as that is frequently when they get fresh ideas for where to go next. But it is the rare artist who takes feedback as instruction. Instead, they persevere with doubts, confidence or compulsion to start again and keep going, to meet us somewhere they will never see. That means that all artists live with failure, too, in the public arena and in their own minds. It's hard to tell which is the tougher test. Rather than trying to second-guess an audience that remains ambiguous and dynamic, the desire for freedom, that strong sense of agency that drove artists in the first place, keeps them going.

The goal isn't, can't be, perfection. 'A perfect poem is impossible', Robert Graves wrote. 'Once it had been written, the world would end.'[16] If a perfect novel were written, a perfect picture painted, why ever make another? There would be no more prospect of discovery. The more modest – but still ambitious – aim is to do better next time. It's why everyone quotes Samuel Beckett: 'Fail better.'

Soweto Kinch recognizes that the music he makes changes him. When he finishes an album, he isn't the same musician who started it. His identity evolves with the music he makes and by the experience that life throws at him along the way.

'I'm capturing the sincere thoughts and feelings of me at one moment in time, at 22 years old, at 25 years old, or my 40s', Kinch said. 'I'm not looking to capture the perfectly formed me, it's more about what's becoming. The idea of perfection along a journey is sort of pernicious and wrong. Accept this point along the journey; it is what it is and if I want it to be better, then that has to be the next thing.'[17]

Instead of pursuing perfection, and often to the outrage or bafflement of their fans, artists change. Gerhard Richter has turned to small, delicate drawings and to huge sculptures in metal and glass. Lubaina Himid now works with textiles and integrates sound into her work. Soweto Kinch moved into rap, working with the London Symphony Orchestra and hosting radio programmes. No two Jeremy Deller projects are remotely the same. Peter Flannery turned to the detective genre, writing eight series of the George Gently stories. Kazuo Ishiguro tried to be a songwriter before he became a novelist – and has now returned to writing songs. Beyoncé has taken up country music and Charles Hazlewood now works with choreographers. The vast range of Richter's work is driven by scepticism; use a successful technique too often, he says, and it starts to look like a trick. But no more than Graves does he believe in perfection, so he keeps looking.

This can come at a cost. Arnold Schoenberg's admirers were appalled when he abandoned the plangent lyricism of 'Verklärte Nacht' for the 12-tone scale, and plenty of James Joyce's staunchest devotees still baulk at *Finnegans Wake*. Many furious Miles Davis fans have never forgiven his electric years and his forays into funk, while it has taken decades for Bob Dylan enthusiasts to appreciate that change is the point, that the developing self is Dylan's subject.

The changes that artists make aren't simple or easy but an energetic expression of driven questioning that may persist until the very end of life. Beethoven's late quartets, Matisse's cut-outs, Rembrandt's self-portraits, Ibsen and Shakespeare's last great poetic works – all bristle with new ideas, exorbitant life and fearless originality. Once, asked how to test for life on Mars, the scientist James Lovelock advised NASA to look for change in the atmosphere. If nothing changes, he said, then the planet is dead. The same might be said of all creative lives.

'If the work has brought you from one place to another', James Baldwin said, 'you've arrived at another point. This then is one's consolation, and you know that you must now proceed elsewhere.'[18]

All this flies in the face of the way that we are routinely urged to think about ourselves: to develop a brand, 'Brand You', turning unique talents into winning but static formulae. The industrialization of self – aided and abetted by apps that can monitor, measure and analyse our every moment, move and mouthful – is the ultimate articulation of a desire that, instead of developing our humanity, with all the fluidity to adapt and respond creatively to uncertainty, we should aim to nail ourselves to the flag of our choice and promote it unwaveringly. It's frightening to think just how absurd and degrading this is. Marx called it reification, the turning of humans into commodities, as though we were all so many detergents jostling for space on a supermarket shelf.

Brands, every marketer will tell you, depend on three things: Consistency. Consistency. Consistency. Branded products sell certainty; a bulwark against change and uncertainty, their appeal is the challenge and discovery they *won't* offer. As such, they are the antithesis of art, the opposite of the meaning, richness and joy that we find in front of a painting, immersed in a book or untethered in a sound cloud of emotion. A brand, the director Peter Brook insisted, is a prison.

Artists have always striven to break out, to move into new genres and disciplines. Michelangelo was a sculptor, a painter, an architect, a poet; Da Vinci is as famous for the profusion of his inventiveness as for any single work. Bursting out of boxes is what creative people do. General Idea's work defies classification. Kae Tempest works as a poet, a non-fiction and fiction author, a playwright, composer and singer. Steve McQueen's work spans Oscars and the Turner Prize. In her installations, Anne Hardy integrates music and smell into her work; her lights connect to live weather stations so that the entire environment brings the outdoors inside. After his Turner-nominated project *RAFTS*, Rory Pilgrim brought out an album, *The Undercurrents*, and has moved on to a feature film – all artists determined to stay out of prison.

That isn't to say there is no consistency in the work of artists, but that it reveals itself only retrospectively. Jane and Louise Wilson didn't set out to be artists of frightening liminal spaces. But *Stasi City* gave rise to a host of ideas and relationships that led them to do works about the Houses of Parliament, Star City outside of Moscow and to Chernobyl in Ukraine.

'Who knew', they laughed, 'that we have a capacity to form relationships with secret hidden places and inanimate things?' But they're quick to dismiss any idea of marketing positioning; they aren't cultivating a Jane and Louise Wilson brand.

'You want certain freedoms', Louise says. 'If you were a brand, how would you achieve that freedom?'

'It would feel very heavy, very quickly', Jane said. 'The life would go out of it.'

Within General Idea, brands were more often a source of irony and absurdity than of inspiration. 'Any time we felt we were in a box' A.A. Bronson told me, 'we'd invent a project that felt like it came from some completely different place or angle. To be successful in the marketplace, you have to be in a box and we could never bear that. I understand the idea of Brand You – it's a very simple idea, but it doesn't coincide with reality. The most interesting people cross boundaries and apply knowledge from one discipline to something completely different, because that is how life is.'

Defying categories can make an artist's work exhilarating. Thomas Laigle started his work in electrical design, chiefly theatre lighting and sound. Then he was drawn to the underground, DIY punk scene, but grew impatient with it; there's nothing so conformist, he said, as the non-conformist. So he experimented with incandescent light bulbs, connecting them to sensors and feeding them through effects pedals to create – what? Light bulb music? Musical light? Because the lights are incandescent, each distorts any regular beat going through them; that's a big part of the pleasure he and his crowds crave – they never know precisely what will emerge. The club scene in Berlin loved it; they'd never seen anything like it before.

But now the light bulbs are becoming obsolete, he knows that his instruments will soon disappear. That gives his music (and it is music, with pitch and rhythm) an energetic poignancy. There is something about Laigle's work that captures the fragile, contingent energy of today: it's exciting, incredible that music can be made this way, and eerily uncomfortable that it will never repeat, or last. But Laigle isn't worrying about brand. He's moving on, now working with dancers, using their bodies as his new instruments.

Nevertheless, the idea of an artist's work becoming recognizable is critical to the business of art; a great deal of both sentimental and financial value comes from the familiarity of images and styles. For artists to live means selling their work, and their galleries often operate within a set of ideas, telling a story through the artists they choose and the exhibitions they mount. As Oliver Evans at the Maureen Paley gallery knows, however, it's not in the nature of art or artists to fit in.

'When I'm looking at an artist's work I'm thinking: what could this be over a five-year period? How do we expand on this thing you're doing? And you have to put faith in this network of people that might come together and formulate a sort of structure for putting something identifiable into the world. But you also know that if an artist has a particular personality and they don't want to conform to someone else's idea, then they can still make the success themselves. …'

After decades of working with artists at the gallery, Evans knows how unpredictable an artist's work is and how vital that uncertainty can be.

'You may take on an artist thinking they're going to go in a particular direction but they rarely stick to the path you might think. Often the surprise is better than anything you might've thought was coming. So you have to be open to that; in the end, nobody really knows what will happen next.'

'Continuity', Caryl Phillips believes, 'is for other people to find. They will tell me what the book is. The author's task is the next book.' Phillips' work encompasses novels about his family's move from St Kitts to England, the African diaspora, an imagining of Emily Brontë, the life of vaudevillian Bert Williams and of the author Jean Rhys, along with essays, journalism and plays. These might seem wildly disparate, but to Phillips, it has an organic logic: 'Eventually you might become aware that there is a space in the forest that you keep revisiting. I know words like home, identity, belonging: I'm in that general area of the forest. But I'm not bothered about how they relate. I just try to concentrate on making something new.'

That artists have such appetite for change is also why they are frequently ahead – that's what *avant garde* means. Making the future in order not to be trapped happens so often that it is considered quasi-magical, a gift, not a plan. Inspiration. Intuition. Emergent. Marketers puzzle over it with envy, oblivious to the fact that it derives from everything that isn't data. When the filmmaker Beeban Kidron made *Oranges Are Not the Only Fruit*, its timeliness was so striking that debates ensued as to how far it had caused greater acceptance of lesbianism or how far it had reflected it. Cause – or effect? Certainly not deliberate; the fact that TV series take years of planning and production makes precision timing impossible to predict or plan. Many of Kidron's films – about sex workers, drag queens and the problems children were experiencing due to the internet – came out years before these were mainstream topics. More even than financial markets, the market for ideas is impossible to time. But artists so often absorb and then reflect the world back to itself that historians turn to them to identify the earliest signals of change.

'You keep one eye on the horizon,' Kidron says, 'you see something and move towards it. You don't know what it will be. Or become. You're cavalier, not strategic. You keep moving forwards. ... I've probably made a lot of interventions that were ahead of their time or bumped into. The moment meets you just as you meet the moment. There is something about leading from within, looking for an articulation of something that has been either unsaid or poorly articulated.'

Whatever the idea, she argues, it is you – but it isn't only about you; rather a strange fusion between the artist, the times, the moods and minds of others and a compelling idea that draws you to take action, again and again.

'Everyone thinks they're an outsider. Outside of something. Culturally that has been seen as a negative, but I see it as a positive: that actually, if you are witness to your own life, to your own community, to your own family, and you take a position as a witness about how you would like to be, it gives you agency, because there's a gap between what is and what could be. And within that gap, you find agency. In those moments, you do feel that you represent a zeitgeist.'

While art and artists remain defiantly fluid and shape-shifting, critics and agents try to place them within neat definitions, categories and ranks. It can be a little perverse – trying to box in artists whose gift is their capacity to seize and use imaginative freedom – but it feeds the public demand for certainty: is this really good? Will it be a waste of my time, my money? Debates on the quality of work most often settle for agreeing that time, not branding, is the test, that excellence is what lasts. But even that verdict remains uncertain too.

The poet John Clare enjoyed enormous fame at the start of his career. In 1820, the success of his first collection, *Poems Descriptive of Rural Life and Scenery*, brought him out of rural Northamptonshire to the dazzle of London society. The Marquess of Exeter granted him an annuity; the public rushed to subscribe to his new publications. But after three years, his rural charm had run its London course and he was nearly broke. Although his last volume, *The Rural Muse*, was well reviewed, it didn't earn him enough money to support his family. Depression and delusions followed, and most of the remainder of his life was spent in Northamptonshire General Lunatic Asylum, crystal clear in his poetry, but in prose or conversation, incomprehensible and forgotten for nearly 100 years.

Yet in the middle of the 20th century, the pure groundedness of his language, even the idiosyncrasy of his punctuation, felt modern. Today his brilliant, expert eye for the natural world comes to us through perfect but simple choices that produce what Seamus Heaney described as 'couplets wound up like clockwork and then sent to scoot merrily through their foreclosed motions. He seemed to write this kind of poem as naturally as he breathed.'[19]

If numbers could measure or predict quality, then for centuries *King Lear* was a flop: rarely performed, mostly forgotten, deemed too dark and miserable to stage – until the post-war period when suddenly it seemed the ultimate articulation of a modern sensibility. The play hadn't changed; we had. For 300 years, Caravaggio was dismissed as vulgar, lewd and impious. One of his greatest paintings – the *Supper at Emmaus* – ended up in the National Gallery only because it failed to sell at auction. Yet today, tourists make pilgrimages to Naples, hoping for the chance to see just three of his pictures. His hookers, hustlers and card sharps are now celebrated for the reality and drama they impart to scenes that feel as accessible as out-takes from movies. And, after all his ambivalence and alterations, Mahler's first symphony is now frequently cited as among his finest work. These works had not changed; the audiences had.

In the 1980s, when much of the world seemed to feel that the drama of the civil rights movement was over, James Baldwin recognized he'd been left behind, forgotten even. Living in France, where Caryl Phillips and I met with him, he was still writing, ever the open-hearted, eloquent analyst of truths and lies, clear-eyed about his own fall from fashion. But even his journalism had never been just about a moment in time. A searing analyst not only of race in the United States but of the cancer he identified at the heart of the American dream, he had always interrogated himself and the world with a bold outsider's eye. His genius was to see as a disease the American need to denigrate groups of 'others' – Black, Gay, Female – in order to feel good about themselves, and he put his finger on why happiness in America required so much effortful consumption. And so his work lay latent, ready for the next century, when America and the world had to confront, again, the fantasies and illusions that perpetuate fury and violence. America needed Baldwin, again.

No brand manager would ever have conceived of reopening Sadler's Wells opera at the end of the Second World War with a piece of such dark complexity and ambiguity as Benjamin Britten's 'Peter Grimes'. 'At first', the critic Edmund Wilson wrote, 'you think that Peter Grimes is Germany ... above all he wants to prove to his neighbors that he is not the scoundrel they think him.' And yet, '... by the time you are done with the opera – or by the time it is done with you – you have decided that "Peter Grimes" is the whole of bombing, machine-gunning, mining, torpedoing, ambushing humanity which talks about a guaranteed standard of living, yet does nothing but wreck its own works, degrade or pervert its own moral life and reduce itself to starvation.'[20] Not for Britten some jingoistic celebration of the triumph of good over evil. Instead, he looked into the century's deepest destructive impulses and the raw experience of violence that his audience had lived through. His genius was that sense of zeitgeist that saw that the propagandist simple binary of the war – good vs evil – merely disguised the ambiguity, anxiety and rage of trauma that his audience had experienced. All performances sold out.

And they still do. Even Edmund Wilson may not have suspected how powerfully this difficult, dark, ambivalent opera would hold its power to this day. An opera about a miserable loner, an abuser of children, despised by his neighbours? How could he have known that child labour, the urge to shame, the violent hatred of crowds would remain so tragically relevant to our own times? Not by chasing fame, but by looking deeply, far and wide.

Art that lasts isn't selling us anything. The historian James Shapiro commented that, search Shakespeare as long as you like, you will find no ideology. What draws us back, again and again, is a rich dialogue between artists and ourselves more intimate and complex than the efficiency that daily life typically affords. And it never really ends. Writing of Joyce and Chekhov, Virginia Woolf observed that their work leaves questions 'to sound on and on after the story is ended ... with a view of infinite possibilities.'

On the day I watched Why Not Theatre perform their *Mahabharata* in London, we had awoken that October morning to news of a war in Gaza. Like the war of the Pandavas and Kauravas, it was shocking in its violence, brutality, scale. As enacted that night, the Indian epic poem spoke as though for the first time of the reductive, binary thinking that Jain and Fernandes had struggled to overcome in themselves. Their dream of finding a way to stage the great poem, that honoured both what it was then and what it is now, came alive fully, tragically, on stage that night. As W.H. Auden wrote of W.B. Yeats, 'The words of a dead man/ Are modified in the guts of the living.'[21]

At every stage of an artist's work, uncertainty lies in wait. In the wandering, the waiting for an idea to gel, in persevering through confusion and disappointment at the bottom of the well. Every choice demands patience and humility too. And when the work is done, the cycle starts again. Surely, a time management guru might insist, this can be streamlined, tested at every stage, rendered more efficient? But if the purpose is merely to finish, why start in the first place? What makes art difficult and demanding is what keeps our attention: it feels like life.

While the finished works of artists may feel exuberant and magical, the activities and processes that go into them are not. In all of us, is (or could be) the capacity to meander and notice, to be where we are and watch what happens around us. An appetite for exploration and experiments, a gift for improvisation – these have been with us for all our history. And without patience and humility we would never have survived. So while most may shy away from the intentional uncertainty of an artist's life, there is much that all of us can learn from it that frees us from the tyranny of efficiency to embrace the spontaneity, complexity and freedoms of real life.

RADA

I did it because Alan Rickman asked me to. 'You need something important to do', he said when I returned to England. So I joined the board. I don't recall now whether it was at my first or second meeting that I became overwhelmed by the sense that something was wrong. I didn't believe what I was being told, felt that the meetings were stage-managed, scripted, that the real action was always offstage. It would make sense, I thought, that what I saw was theatre.

Alan and I discussed my misgivings, then met with two board members whom we trusted. We all started paying more attention: to contradictions, vacuities and obliquities, ducking and dodging. Finances were scrutinized like never before. It didn't feel good that, as we grew more inquisitive, the management team became more defensive.

Half the board were businesspeople and half artists, mostly RADA graduates. It sounds fun, but it wasn't much. Overwhelmed by business jargon, the actors would pull back. The business folk were wary of them; fearing the performers were too fragile and oversensitive, they tiptoed around important topics, not wanting to throw their weight around. Stereotyping and politely misunderstanding one another produced a mutually assured stalemate. Fear of conflict maintained a grim status quo.

A board awayday arrived, ably chaired by a former union negotiator. Lots of the usual stuff: discussions of what it meant to be a drama school, the tension between accepting pretty students versus the ones who looked like life. Then finance. A lot of evasion and bland assurances when, finally, from Sylvia Syms, once known as the Grande Dame of British Cinema, came the unmistakably regal tones of a great actor: 'Do you mean to say … [careful, heavy, pause] that the Royal Academy of Dramatic Art is going *bust*?'

At last. Someone with no fear of conflict, and we could begin the real conversation. Not because the business experts demanded it, but because the artists had seen through the weasel words and flimsy explanations. It struck me then, and it strikes me still, that the actors around the table were tougher and braver, and better able to interpret what they said and heard, than the executives who imagined themselves leaders. Accustomed to conflict, actors knew how to handle it – that was their stock-in-trade – while the businessmen and women were afraid of it, craving order and imagining actors too unworldly to bear reality. And yet, in that one dramatic moment, the board finally became as one: facing the truth and coming together to address the crisis. Not a moment too soon.

1. *Aunt Marianne*, oil on canvas, Gerhard Richter, 1965

2. *Sky Sketch*, from *The 'Skies' Sketchbook*, watercolour, J.M.W. Turner, 1816–18

3. *Raby Castle*, watercolour, J.M.W. Turner, 1817

4. *Trip the Light Fantastic*, Paraorchestra at Bristol Beacon,
photograph, Paul Blakemore, 2023

5. *Trip the Light Fantastic*, Paraorchestra at Bristol Beacon,
photograph, Paul Blakemore, 2023

6. *FILE Magazine* front cover, Special General Idea Issue, vol 5, no 4, 1983

7. *Imagevirus*, from the series *Imagevirus*, poster, General Idea, 1989

8 and 9. *Stasi City*, video stills, exhibition by Jane and Louise Wilson, 1997,
Metropolitan Museum of Art, New York, 2018–19

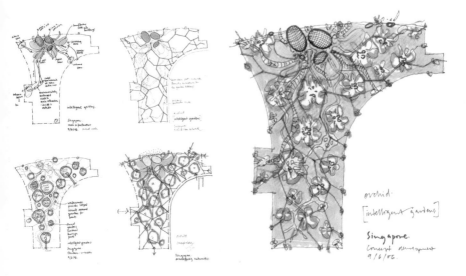

10. *A Vision of Singapore*, Gardens by the Bay,
map from the Bay South booklet, Daniel Soh

11. *World Orchid Festival*, Gardens by the Bay,
photograph from the Bay South booklet, Daniel Soh

12–14. *Painting the Bird at Electricity Tower, Grottaglie*, wall art, Lucy McLauchlan, artist and Matthew Watkins, photographer, Fame Festival Italy, 2009

15. *Night Journey*, acrylic on canvas, Frank Bowling, 1969–70

16. *Enges Bretterhaus/Narrow Stage*, Cibachrome mounted, Rut Blees Luxemburg, 1998

17. *Red Box*, photograph, Christian Hagemann

18. *American People Series #20: Die*, oil on canvas, Faith Ringgold, 1967

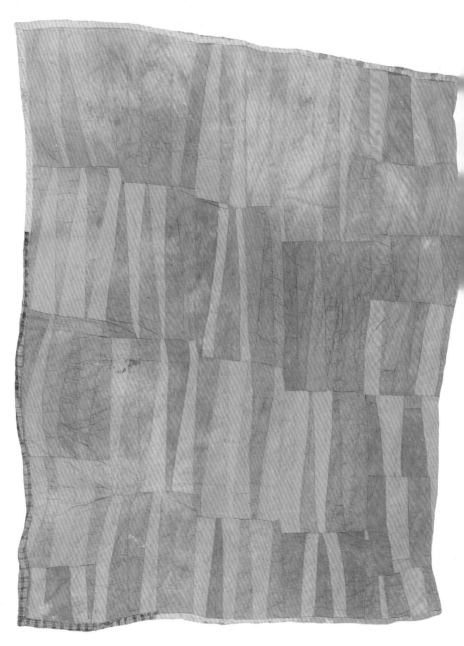

19. *String-Pieced Quilt*, cotton twill and synthetic material (men's clothing), Loretta Pettway, 1960

20. *Dancing on the Silos*, photograph, Raissa Page, Greenham Common, 1 January 1983

21. *Greenham Common*, photograph, Maggie Murray, Format Photographers

22. Women for Peace: Banners from Greenham Common, *"Coercion Is Not Government"*, *Sylvia Pankhurst, Then or Now*, Thalia Campbell, 1985

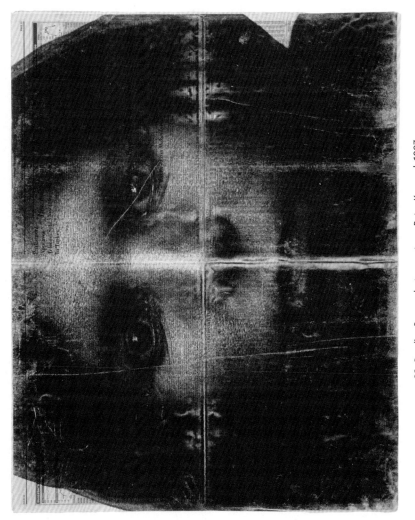

23. *Reading Room*, photo montage, Peter Kennard, 1997

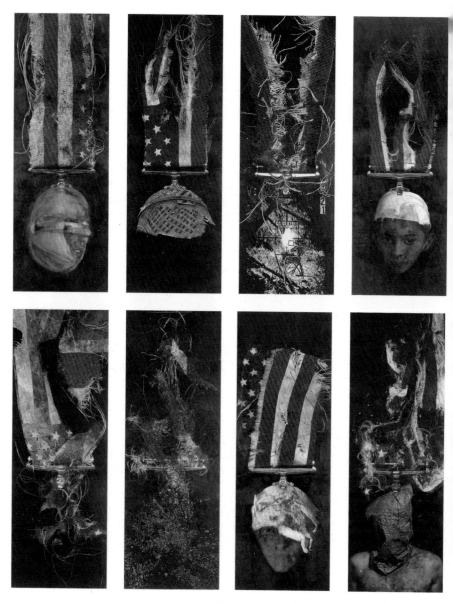

24. *Decoration*, painting, Peter Kennard, 2003

4

Prepared minds

Curiosity. Patience. Courage. An eye for detail. Stamina. Minds open and alert to alternatives. A love of discovery. The ability to live with paradox. A bringer-together of utterly disparate people, places and ideas: in an age of uncertainty, of polycrisis and systemic collapse, these are the capabilities and mindsets we need everywhere we turn. In our politics: as they become violent and brittle, we need people who can notice, inhabit, understand and communicate complex truths. In our daily lives: as the social fabric frays, we depend on people who can manage conflict with grace and stamina, appreciating that it is at the intersection of ideas and paradoxes that new paths emerge. In organizations striving for innovative thinking and action to tackle climate change, disease, migration, social incohesion and inequalities, people who can think like artists are essential. This is urgent. For at least two decades now, we have seen that obedient, efficient, predictable, linear thinking won't work; that more, even better, of the same won't get us out of the mess we are in.

Which makes it astonishing that, in much of the world, the arts are cut back, denigrated, trivialized and marginalized, just as we need them the most. In the UK, between 2010 and 2022, the number of students taking GCSEs in arts subjects fell by 40 per cent, with design and technology down by 71 per cent, media and film down 50 per cent and performance and expressive arts down 65 per cent. At A-level, overall arts subjects are down 28 per cent and design by 60 per cent.[1]

In the UK and the US, much of this decline can be explained by what can only be described as educational panic – a belief that maintaining global economic dominance depends on STEM subjects (Science, Technology, Engineering and Mathematics) to the exclusion of all else. In 2010, as minister for education, Michael Gove introduced the EBacc (English Baccalaureate), a performance measure of schools and students, based on the percentage who pass GCSEs in 'core' subjects, which 'are considered essential to many degrees and open up a lot of doors. ...'[2] The EBacc did not include any arts subjects.[3]

In 2016, the trend accelerated with the introduction of Progress 8 scores. These are designed to measure how far a student improves over a five-year period compared to a government-calculated level of expected improvement; they are supposed to demonstrate how big a difference each school has made. Again, the arts aren't counted. So those who want to do arts subjects won't push a school up the league tables. It's a deliberate way to steer teachers, children (and their parents) away from the arts altogether.

These novel policies go a long way towards explaining why participation in arts subjects has fallen precipitately, and why it is now possible to visit primary schools where you won't hear a single instrument being played. In 2018, art history disappeared altogether as an A-level subject. Government ads featuring a ballet dancer and suggesting that 'Fatima's next job could be in cyber (she just doesn't know it yet)' said it all: ballet is a waste of time; do something practical, measurable, profitable.[4]

In university funding, political antipathy to the arts is even more evident. In 2021, the UK government's Department for Education cut the undergraduate subsidy for subjects in the performing and creative arts, together with media studies, by 49 per cent – at a time when applications to study these subjects reached their highest level in a decade.[5]

Such a concerted effort to downgrade arts subjects has largely been driven by two beliefs. The first (conflating society with the economy) assumes that society will thrive if we just fix the economy, so all education needs to do is manufacture the right workers. It's a strangely anti-educational solution: the idea that reducing curriculum makes it better, alongside the magical belief that we know exactly what the future needs. Stranger still when we acknowledge our urgent need for innovation. The second article of faith, endemic to bureaucracies, is the insistence that everything that matters can be measured and that measurement is the hallmark of accountability. There are all kinds of problems with this, not least that the easiest system to measure is one that has been designed specifically *to be* measured. Instead of creating the richest, most adaptable learning system and assessing that, curriculum and content have been designed for measurability.[6] Metrics can always be expected to produce unintended consequences, but those are routinely overlooked or underestimated in favour of the certainty numbers purport to provide.

That measurement has become so central to educational thinking means that it now percolates straight down from Whitehall to teachers and students, all of whom go into school each day with measurement front of mind. Teachers teach to tests, in part because that is how their own performance, as well as that of the whole school, is measured. Students absorb the lesson, to do as they are told and focus on the grades instead of developing their native curiosity and initiative. Perhaps the most striking example I've found was an eight-year-old girl, whose class was assigned a project about the Amazon rainforest over the spring school break. Using an old camping tent, she created a mock-up of the forest, complete with papier mâché animals, birds and plants and a sound-track of Amazonian wildlife. Everyone else knew the drill; their higher marks were for cutting and pasting Wikipedia articles into a binder. The young girl was chastised for being too creative and marked down because her project didn't contain enough text.

She had fallen foul of criterion-based assessment, a method of judging a student's work by comparing it to a set of predetermined standards and criteria. In other words, it assigns no value to creativity, but merely measures how far the student has matched what someone, somewhere has already decided is the 'right' answer. This process was introduced in the late 1980s (along with the national curriculum) in the hope that it would be fair – and many will say that it is fairer than marking to a curve. But in assessing a student's thinking by how closely it conforms to the predetermined correct response, it specifically teaches them *not* to think for themselves. The process is all about fitting to a model and does nothing to reward initiative, ingenuity, independent thinking or anything not on the menu of the approved answer. No wonder so many bosses complain to me that their highly credentialled workforce consists primarily of expert second-guessers, pleasers, not thinkers. It's a terrible thing to do to young minds, leaving them utterly unprepared for uncertainty, change and innovation.

The story in the United States is roughly similar, where for decades standardized, multiple-choice testing has been the norm. Again, this rewards knowing the right answer rather than the capacity to consider a range of feasible possibilities. These militate against discursive thinking, but perhaps not nearly so profoundly as the eye-watering cost of university education in the United States, which leaves most American graduates terrified of studying subjects that don't promise immediate financial rewards. Teachers across the country complain of arts and humanities subjects having 'fallen off a cliff' at universities: students majoring in humanities declined by 37 per cent in the 10 years between 2012 and 2022.[7]

In both the US and the UK, the focus on a narrow range of testable subjects is defended with the argument that the Western economies don't need arts or humanities graduates; they need more engineers. But framing this as binary is a mistake; it isn't (or shouldn't be) a question of either one or the other. In the US, a plethora of research studies have demonstrated that engagement in arts activities improved achievement in *all* other subjects. The thinking developed by looking at, interpreting and discussing a painting, for example, transfers to analysing cells or graphs, clothing or food. Music and mathematics appear to strengthen one another. Doing drama improves reading and understanding narrative. When the Brookings Institution undertook the first ever large-scale, randomized controlled trial study of a city's efforts to restore arts education, they found that students in schools with enhanced arts funding developed much greater enthusiasm and engagement for their school work and were able to think in new ways. These students also exhibited greater compassion for others. None of this came at the expense of other subjects; writing improved and disciplinary infractions fell.[8]

A vast compendium of studies shows that verbal and maths skills, social and thinking skills are developed by the arts, as is that most fundamental of attitudes: motivation to learn.[9]

The pace of change and the social and intellectual demands that uncertainty places on everyone – students and citizens alike – has become a live issue in many Irish universities too. How can they help their students manage this volatility without devaluing quality and tradition? How to help them develop relationships, not just the ability to transact? In an unscripted world, what will help young people face their future unafraid to explore, experiment, challenge and discover areas rich with ambiguity? This doesn't mean traditional learning – the deep knowledge of a single subject – doesn't matter; it acknowledges that work-defined skills alone are inadequate for civil society. Within Irish universities, such questions have led to an emphasis on 'transversal skills': the capacity for ethical, creative and critical thinking, because life is more complex than binary or tick-box choices allow, and is full of unforeseen, non-linear consequences. Why do they call these 'transversal skills'? Because that's what they are – capable of enhancing every other capacity – but also because educationalists know that naming them 'soft skills' not so subtly undermines their value.[10]

Fanatical focus on a narrow range of eminently testable subjects is defended with the argument that it's the only way to drive economic growth. It's not an obvious or particularly well-informed conclusion to come to. Nor is a narrower curriculum characteristic of high-achieving school systems. The global PISA (Programme for International Student Assessment) tests started in 2000 with the goal of benchmarking educational achievement around the world, in order to understand which approaches best enhance student learning. It is not designed to make countries compete with one another, but to understand what drives rising educational attainment, so that all societies can learn from it. Education in Singapore has been widely admired for the country's performance in the PISA – but what that means is often misunderstood or out of date. That this small, young country has done so well is not due to a relentless, competitive focus on standardized tests, but to the awareness that what underpinned the country's first 50 years of success would not be sufficient for the next 50.

'Several years ago, we were trying to move from exams as the sole criteria for success', Thiam Seng Koh told me. A leading educationalist in Singapore's Ministry of Education, he was concerned by how rigid schools had become. 'So we went to New York for inspiration. To our horror, they'd gone in the other direction, they were trying to move to where we are! The old kind of education just helped kids work to a formula. But if the average guys are just working to the formula, we will be dead in no time. The world is just changing too fast.'

Instead, Koh initiated programmes that brought art and the sciences together to develop capacity far beyond the ability to second-guess teachers and examiners. Using an approach called 'Teach Less, Learn More', Singapore educators found ways to put more white space into the timetable to enhance art and music offerings and to develop curiosity and a love of play. He aimed to make students feel less like machines accepting a download, and more like young thinkers.

'In this work, there's a lot of debate, rebuttal, disagreement. You need students to challenge you to get innovation and creativity.' These changes marked a big cultural shift for Singaporeans and was, Koh conceded, very challenging, not least when his own son decided to give up biology.

'There was a ruckus in the classroom: what signal are you trying to send? But that is the signal I am trying to send. Now he's enjoying himself. He has more free periods, he plays his guitar. He can make some of his own choices.'

As the demands of society and global economies change, PISA has continued to evolve. In 2015, PISA added tests addressing students' capacity to work collaboratively. In 2022, for the first time, they set out to gauge how far schools were developing students' creative thinking, which was defined as 'the ability to generate, evaluate and improve ideas to produce original and effective solutions, advance knowledge and create impactful expressions of imagination.'[11] Why measure creative thinking? Because it 'can have a positive influence on students' academic interest and achievement, identity and socio-emotional development', and because that capacity is fundamental to 'the investigation of issues, problems or society-wide concerns.'[12]

The research showed that all students have the potential to think creatively; doing so requires self-efficacy, an openness to art and new experiences, imagination and adventurousness, curiosity, the capacity to see different perspectives and persistence. Sound familiar?

Girls were shown to be considerably stronger creative thinkers than boys, 'because they show more positive beliefs about creativity, feel more imaginative and open to perspective taking.'[13] Those characteristics, combined with greater curiosity, openness to intellect and persistence, are associated with stronger creative thinking. Students who think their creativity is something they can change *for themselves* (a sense of agency) outscored those who believed otherwise, and academic excellence was not shown to be a prerequisite, although neither was it a hindrance.

On creative thinking, Singapore came top of the PISA list. Korea, Canada, Australia, New Zealand, Estonia and Finland followed, in descending order. But the US and the UK opted out of this assessment. Creative thinking? They didn't want to know.

That PISA saw a connection between agency and creativity wasn't a new discovery; it merely validates what we know about the importance of intrinsic motivation. Students who are driven by their own curiosity and creativity, who delight in exploring and inventing – like the girl making her miniature rainforest – frequently roam far beyond the narrow confines of a specified task. That freedom confirms and energizes their sense of self, their independence and agency. Creativity quickly becomes self-perpetuating.

Allowing the mind to wander, to notice, is a form of learning, and there is powerful evidence that it makes young people mentally more adaptable; they develop prepared minds better able to adjust to new circumstances. Conversely, inadequate time to play, to reflect and daydream can have negative consequences for emotional wellbeing and the ability to pay attention. Mind wandering isn't sloppy and it isn't lazy; high levels of imagination are correlated with self-control, not the reverse.[14]

The motivating factor *is* pleasure: delight in exploration, in discovering new ways to share knowledge, in mastering a complicated project that, at times, seemed too difficult. Intrinsic motivation generates its own energy, commitment, independence and discipline long after any grade is forgotten. This is not only true of young people; it's a lifelong gift. You could call Piers Plowright the epitome of intrinsic motivation.

The extrinsically motivated student, by contrast, is all about tactics. Learning isn't the point; the grade is. What parent hasn't heard the refrain 'I don't need to know that; it isn't on the test'? All children start life curious, but that sentence spells its death as the sheer grind of constant assessment reduces learning to a need-to-know process. Once curiosity and agency die, incentives – grades, pay rises, perks – must step in. Their biggest problem isn't that they don't work, but that they do. If the grade is all that matters, who cares how it's achieved? Cheating, plagiarism, performance-enhancing drugs like Adderall or Ativan can seem easier options.[15] What the student doesn't develop – initiative, delight, a growing sense of achievement and identity – risks becoming a very long-term cost of an ostensibly efficient system.

We don't know the specific disciplines and skills that the future will demand or value. We do know that we will need the capacities artists bring to their work. Katie Paterson's infinite curiosity. The fertile openness of Jeremy Deller. Peter Flannery's stamina. Anne Hardy's deep observation and sense making. Andrew Grant's inventive ambition. Lubaina Himid's courage. Jed Mercurio's heightened awareness of the world. Rut Blees Luxemburg's self-critique. Kae Tempest's capacity for change. All artists' ability to support, and be supported by, others. That's why Koh takes his son's fun seriously. Finding what he loves is how the young man will identify work that energizes him and drives him to seek new challenges. Making his own choices and feeling their consequences is essential to developing creative confidence, accountability, and with it, anticipatory creativity. In a volatile, unpredictable world, an education devoid of such capabilities leaves us helpless, passive and lost.

And yet, still the perception that the arts are soft, irrelevant, useful only as hobbies, persists as defunding accelerates. 'It's like dessert', Soweto Kinch said to me with frustration. 'Delicious. Unnecessary. Probably bad for you.' He spoke for most artists who are aghast at how far arts funding in the UK has been slashed over the last decade. Nationally, funding per person has been reduced by 33 per cent in Scotland, 36 per cent in Wales and 50 per cent in England in real terms. In addition, local authorities, who also bear much of the financial costs of the arts, austerity has been brutal, with cuts equivalent to 23 per cent per person.[16] Councils including Bury, Bolton and Tower Hamlets have had to sell art in their collections simply to stay afloat.[17] In addition, funding to libraries has fallen by 54 per cent, leading to the closure of 800 (180 since 2016) and 467 museums have been lost since 2000.[18] The BBC, the largest cultural institution in the UK, which supports artists, musicians, writers, designers – many at the critical early stages of their careers – has lost a quarter of its funding. In the United States, the total budget for the National Endowment for the Humanities is now roughly the same size as that of the Vienna State Opera – and there are those who would prefer it was zero.[19]

Like cancer, the illness can be hard to spot. Visit London's West End and it looks vibrant enough. But these theatres, with their hit shows, draw from talent that was inspired, developed and trained 20 to 50 years ago. The schools, museums, concert halls and local repertory theatres that brought young people into the arts, as practitioners and audiences, are now significantly weakened, or simply gone. Like a body that is malnourished for years, the environment from which the dynamism of British cultural life drew its vitality is now frail, expending dwindling resources to look like it is still alive. But with an education system energetically discouraging new blood, it's becoming increasingly difficult to see where the next generation will come from. As any cancer patient knows, looking healthy is a far cry from being healthy. And the arrival of a new government doesn't guarantee a last-minute cure.

While governments routinely assume that artists can live on air, the mundane reality is that they don't; they stagger on, doing low-paid jobs. It's the rare artist whose livelihood is supported entirely by their art. In the UK, for example, visual artists are among the lowest earning workers in the creative industry, their total median annual income being £12,500, of which just £2,000 comes from their art practice.[20] Low pay is not just demoralizing and denigrating, but risks killing off a once vibrant, diverse and healthy ecosystem, capable of reflecting society, leaving the arts as the part-time playground for a tiny, unrepresentative minority of the well off and their progeny.

The defunding of the arts is not just a matter for those working in it. Going to concerts, plays and museums refreshes and challenges our sense of the world and our place in it, compelling us to consider experiences different from our own, providing a structure within which to understand the world from the perspectives of others. An undogmatic mindset helps us seek, and find, fresh ideas when we are stuck. Essential to a civic society, it's where and how we learn more about our past and where we frequently glimpse the future.[21] Without it, we are isolates, limited by our own experience, constrained by individual history, lacking insight or influence in the world we inhabit.

Defenders of the arts have been vocal and active in arguing its economic value, hoping to persuade efficient self-optimizers that joy, discovery and imagination serve utilitarian purposes. Income derived from all the arts in the UK in 2022 was £109 billion, more than twice the income of pharmaceutical, aerospace and automotive industries *combined*.[22] That number underestimates the arts' true impact as it doesn't include industries like tourism, which thrives when films, TV shows and music make people want to visit the country. Nor does it take into account that almost every object consumers own – from a toothbrush to a car – has been shaped by a designer and sold on a website or in a store designed by an artist. And the creative industries are dynamic, growing 6.9 per cent in the year September 2021–22, while the economy as a whole grew just 1.2 per cent. Imagine: an industry loved by contributors and audiences both, that grows and benefits other industries as well as the population overall.

The argument that the arts are somehow bad for you – decadent and unhealthy – has been countered by mounting evidence that it is mentally and physically good for you.[23] For young people, daily reading reduces hyperactivity and inattention and develops empathy. The same is true of dance, music or art lessons. Adolescents who participate in book clubs, dance, bands or orchestras develop a greater sense of autonomy and personal growth, and they are less likely to take up smoking and drinking or become involved in anti-social or criminal activity. Researchers aren't quite sure why developing their imagination, creativity and problem-solving skills (the everyday life of an artist) has positive benefits, but are persuaded that those skills make a positive difference: enhancing self-esteem, self-control and giving young people a better sense of themselves as actors in their own lives. At a time when digital addiction exacerbates isolation and vulnerability, art offers essential human confirmation.

The same is true for adults, with frequent participation in the arts associated with less mental distress and happier lives – independent of background, income, medical history, demographics or personality. Reading books doesn't just help restore our shattered powers of concentration; it keeps us better informed about the world, and develops our capacity to think about people not like ourselves.[24] At work, our capacity to collaborate effectively depends more on empathy than on IQ.[25] Standing in the shoes of others fine-tunes social understanding, a vital development if we are to withstand polarization and extremism. Different parts of our brain are engaged as we consider scenes, characters and mental states; our imagination – remember that? – is rekindled.[26] Empathy, communication and concentration might seem intangible goods, but they are the foundation of social cohesion, without which everything from the economy to global standing in the world falls apart.

Choirs famously reduce bad moods and stress levels and boost the immune system. Even virtual choirs, where you sing along to an online conductor, have a similar, if weaker, effect. For young mothers, carers and the bereaved, the arts can be a godsend, reducing anxiety and raising levels of self-esteem and self-efficacy. I remember one Somerset project that offered a crèche and a painting class for new mothers; it was one of very few approaches that reduced postnatal depression so successfully that when its funding was cut, the mothers took over running the project for themselves.

These benefits last a lifetime. For the elderly, the arts seems to kick off, or perpetuate, a virtuous cycle. More involvement in the arts makes older people feel better, so they participate more. The consequence is fewer long and chronic diseases, a lower rate of depressive symptoms and obesity. Even when taking into account a wide variety of factors (demographics, socioeconomic background, personality, past medical history, past life experiences, and previous arts and cultural engagement), adults over the age of 50 who visited a theatre, concert or historic building every few months had a 32 per cent lower risk of depression over a period of 10 years; if the visits were monthly, the risk was nearly cut in half. Confronting the greatest terror for older people – dementia – is considerably less terrifying if they attend cultural events every few months, as they suffer less memory loss and maintain greater verbal fluency. And as a group, they live longer.

Yet all these arguments so frequently fall on deaf ears that the problem cannot be one of evidence or argument. It is one of mindset. What this research points to is one thing: whether as participant or audience, the arts produce experience, and that changes you, both literally and figuratively. Your brain and your mind. What you believe. How you think. What you think. How you relate to other people. They keep you capable of change. In an age of uncertainty, when we can't predict what will happen next, we need creativity, communication and resilience to keep going together, and we need imagination, courage and well-stocked minds to be able to adapt. But increasingly that is not what politicized education systems or the market provides.

At a business conference in Oxford, when talking to a group of senior executives in the communications industry, I heard huge frustration at the lack of initiative, creative and critical thinking they found in their young employees. Too needy for precise instructions. Unimaginative. Stymied by unforeseen problems. Rigid in their thinking because, like exams, they expected one right answer and were paralysed and demoralized if they found many or none. Frightened to risk a fresh idea or challenge, they looked primarily for what the bosses wanted.

When I discussed the problem with the president and provost of University College London (UCL), one of the world's top universities, he knew exactly what I meant, linking it straight back to criterion-based assessment. It might be fairer, he thought, than putting people on a curve, but the problem was that it assumes that there is just one right answer. 'It starts from the wrong end of the problem', he said. 'And it assumes that the assessors know that one right answer. That is rarely true of real life.'

In his previous role as vice chancellor of the University of Sydney, every student had the opportunity to be part of a multidisciplinary team with a company, or an organization serving civil society, working on a complex problem: 'You could have

50 different teams working on the problem, with academics from all kinds of disciplines. And in the end, companies would often adopt one of the solutions, for a whole host of reasons you might not have seen or agree with.'

'It was meaningful to the students and to the companies, because it's *not* about knowing the solution beforehand, or doing what everyone else has already done. I think a lot more open-ended educational activity is desirable – and doing it much earlier on, because right now too much of their education is just about getting people to jump through hoops.'

'It is always a mistake to reduce funding for humanities. A mistake, because we need a balanced education, producing people who are both literate and numerate to face the uncertainty of the fourth Industrial Revolution.'

•　•　•

One way to start addressing the issue is to work with artists themselves. At the Gates Foundation, Kathy Kahn recognized that traditional leadership training would get participants nowhere near the capabilities they needed for their WAVE programme to succeed. The West African Virus Epidemiology project's goal is to make the African plant system resilient to climate change and disease. Cassava, a critical crop throughout the continent, is threatened by viruses, some of which are already starting to spread west to east; their reaching East Africa would spell disaster. So the programme aims to prevent that. But while most of the people working on it are scientists, the science may be the easiest part of the project.

The hard part is preparing multiple governments to respond fast and to act together. Epidemiological modellers, scientists, policy makers, local officials and farmers on the ground in West and Central Africa all need to learn a lot about each other's disciplines. That will take patience, a capacity to imagine potential scenarios, face into what could go right or wrong, and to understand what the programme means for people who are very different from one another. As is characteristic of many complex problems, multiple forms of expertise are needed, but no single one can dominate. In confronting a virus that respects nobody, all the scientists have knowledge and influence, but nobody has the power to control what happens next. The complex uncertainties intrinsic to the WAVE programme compelled Kahn to reach beyond the typical executive training programme.

'You have to engage with the whole system', Kahn told me, 'and that was a huge challenge for this team. We really wanted to know that governments were going to put response plans in place – otherwise, why do it? But we had people, the directors of their institutes, who didn't even know what governments were doing, because they were kind of shy plant virologists, you know, immersed in their research. Excellent – but science is not enough. You may understand the threat, but countries have to be prepared to respond *before* it hits – and it hasn't hit Nigeria yet. So that means you have to engage with farmers, donors, government ministers, plant health authorities and scientists. That's complex and it is very different from doing science.'

That's why Kahn pushed for the Foundation to work with Richard Olivier and his Henry V executive programme. She and Olivier had worked together in the past, and she believed his use of Shakespeare could give the WAVE group an experience that could hugely, and quickly, expand their capabilities, their sense of themselves and what they would be able to achieve. Nobody wanted a stack of PowerPoint slides, some bureaucratic tips and coaching tricks. To be successful, the group needed to go much deeper. Given the sheer difficulty of their task, how could the scientists reconceive their mission not as a job, with its tedium and bureaucracy, but as an epic and perilous story?

WAVE's executive director, Justin Pita, knew his team needed help. The programme had to work from top down, but also bottom up, to galvanize both grassroots and institutional support, and fast, before crisis struck. 'The science is the easy part', Pita said. 'Because we are scientists. But we are not experts in managing programmes. Or working with ministers. Or farmers. We had to change our way of doing things, to step out of our comfort zone. And that felt, well, really uncomfortable', he laughed.

Watching scenes from *Henry V* and talking about its characters (especially the newly minted King) gave the scientists a safe way to watch leadership in action, to imagine themselves in each character's shoes, and to explore together what they might do in analogous situations. What kind of leader will Henry become; what kind of leaders did they need to be? Who will help Henry and why? How could they help each other? The story provides a mirror, Olivier says, that others can look at without apparently looking at themselves. As he and a small band of actors worked through extracts of the play, they teased out the different decisions, personalities, options and motives that shape leadership, and encouraged the WAVE scientists to apply it to themselves. None of them were actors so they were nervous, tentative, and that shared anxiety gave the team a sense of solidarity. In a perilous place together, everyone was uncertain about the process. But intrigued.

In Act 3, on invading France, Henry experiences first success, then failure. As a leader, he must be able to speak honestly about both; he senses boosterism will damage his authority. Success in negotiating with the French buys him time, but then he changes strategy, allowing his troops to recover from their first engagement. Henry has to balance justice with mercy, truth with loyalty: tests all decision makers face. He can't be certain of what he does; he's learning as he goes. Soliloquies proved eloquent reminders of the need for solitude: to be able to have a conversation with yourself and find out what you really think, where your feelings tend and where you might be going wrong. These aren't experiences the scientists were used to having, with themselves or with others.

When the group reached Act 4, the biologists could identify with a king facing his fears, knowing how many lives can be affected by a single decision. The Act starts with the Chorus setting the scene. The English soldiers are preparing to die. Henry walks among his men, his 'little touch of Harry in the night', helping them to feel valued, but giving no hint of how vast an army surrounds them. Alone, he is full of misgivings, keenly aware how little power he has to determine the outcome. Is his the right course of action? Does he have what it takes to decide? All leaders have doubt; soliloquies are a window on the mind, letting us see how doubt drives thinking. These scenes caused the group deep reflection, to imagine in personal detail the relationships they need to build, the parts of the system they don't yet understand, the human cost of failure. Instead of denying or burying doubt and fear, the play helped them surface and address them.

When I first met Kahn and heard about her collaboration with Olivier, I was a little sceptical of this application of theatre to business, wary that it might be a fancy form of communications training, a nice experience but with no real staying power. Olivier has taught at Harvard Business School and twice been invited to speak at Davos – always following great crises – but was this (as often happens) a light piece of programming to leaven an otherwise heavyweight agenda? I could see how *Hamlet* and *The Tempest* might relate to leadership, but the choice of *Henry V* initially antagonized me; war as a metaphor for business has always seemed crass, macho, alienating and wrong. But Kahn and Pita's enthusiasm, together with their frank avowal of just how uncertain they had been at the beginning, won me over. Their mission was simply too important, complex and urgent, their commitment and expertise too profound, for them to waste time on anything less than essential. And developing in 'shy biologists' the capacity to deal with stakeholders from farmers to government and tribal leaders was essential if the science was to bestow the benefit for which it had been developed.

Although the science and circumstances of WAVE are unique, the challenge Kahn and Pita faced is not. To get ahead of the virus requires understanding it in huge detail, but also grasping the ecosystem in which it thrives. Being able to craft experiments and develop pilot programmes demands imagination and courage. Invention and reinvention take a lot of mental wandering around, glimpsing fruitful ideas, seeing where they fall down, but not giving up. Understanding other perspectives, in an urgent situation, will need curiosity, together with patience and finely tuned observational skills. Well-stocked minds will provoke doubts, conflict, constant questions that sharpen insight. When things go wrong, everyone will need stamina and resilience to persevere and reimagine, as well as the ability to change – all skills and capacity that the biologists didn't typically learn at school and that has been no part of their scientific or executive education. So while the impact of WAVE is measurable, the qualities on which its success depends are not. That is why Kahn wanted the team to work with Olivier: to get from theatre an experience of the skills and aptitudes that leading through uncertainty requires.

It would be wrong to think that Kahn and the shy biologists represent a special case. In every sector of the economy, I encounter leaders of organizations who struggle to find just those qualities that the WAVE team hopes to learn with Olivier. Employers often can't quite put their fingers on what is missing in their people, but they feel it and know it matters.

'They're bright,' one CEO told me, 'it's like they don't have minds of their own. They come with great grades from good universities. But they only feel comfortable doing what they've been told. And I worry about them. Of course they want to succeed, to be promoted, climb the ladder. But they aren't flexible, adaptive, independent enough to do their own thinking. And by the time they're 35, I don't think they're going to make it. I don't know what they will be able to do then.'

Not one of the many executives with whom I've had such conversations think their people are poorly educated; they all have plenty of qualifications. But they have little experience of ambiguity, creative conflict, getting lost and finding the way through; the strictly defined curricula of their schools and universities ensure this. Working with young leaders hoping to reinvent cities, I was moved and not a little surprised when several approached me, outside of our workshop, to ask how to have a conversation. It was a touching request for help. These were well-schooled, bright, ambitious individuals; I felt confident they were excellent at passing exams, but beginning a conversation that might go anywhere: that intimidated them. And yet without that, they can't initiate the change they so desire for their future.

Working through key scenes and themes in *Henry V* gave the WAVE team the ability to step outside themselves and see the arc of their project, each stage presenting different problems, the end of which could be a safer, healthier Africa. In analysing the characters, they started to see how others might analyse them. Many high achievers reach their high positions by being excellent followers, but now these scientists could experience at a deeper level what it really felt like to be a leader – to know that you don't know when the moment for a decision is ripe, if it is right or wrong, to embrace uncertainty without losing the capacity for action. The play did what all art does: provide a context from which to look differently at oneself and the world, to see afresh through the perspectives and lived experience of others.

Toggling between the drama and their own work, the story began to take on a life that was part Shakespeare, part WAVE. Before the week finished, each participant had to make a closing speech to their colleagues, imagining success. Pita and Kahn made theirs as though to the ministers they would have to persuade.

'Just working on those speeches,' Pita told me, 'I realized that in Benin and Gabon, yes we would be dealing with ministers and the speech helped me feel really prepared for that. But also, I suddenly realized that, in other parts of Africa, we would have to deal with traditional rulers – because it is to those rulers that the ministers will turn. And those kings stay in power far longer, so they were really important. So we couldn't treat everyone the same way, just because we needed their support. ...'

Pita and Kahn talked a lot about how to win the allies the project needed. Who they could trust to tell the truth, to be reliable – all those problems of power. With the WAVE team they discussed openly what it was, individually and collectively, that they would have to overcome and change.

Did it, I wondered, change the way in which the scientists approached the ministers? At this point in our conversation, Pita seemed to light up. All his previous management training, he said, had been instrumental and impossible to remember. But these stories, and the conversations and exercises that accompanied them, were unforgettable; the experience had become part of who he was now. It changed how he felt about the entire project and, in reframing the complexity of the mission, turned him from a shy biologist into a compelling evangelist.

'Justin became so much freer, much more self-assured' Kahn observed. 'It was the way he spoke about the work – well, everyone *wanted* to listen. They were as excited as he was. Ministers, rulers, wanted to help him because he so passionately brought home what the work meant, what it was for.'

Kahn may have commissioned the training for the African virologists, but there were rich lessons in it for her, too. Her own role entailed far more than science, or management, or even a combination of the two: 'I started thinking about directors, and how they work. Part of what they do is they make it okay for people to experiment. They encourage people to take risks and I think that is so important in creativity: to let down inhibitions.'

But what most struck home for Pita was the last Act of the play, which is more remembered for its comedy – Henry V's terrible French as he woos the Princess – than for depth. Actually the Act is about the need for change. Henry is victorious, but if he remains a warrior, the 'garden of France' that he has won will be destroyed. Leaders must keep changing, to adapt to the consequences that emerge from their decisions; the work is never finished.

'It was a simple play, we were together laughing, but it really stays in your mind: that after winning the war you have to win the peace', Pita said. 'It's easy; you don't have to take your book and remind yourself, it's just there. It made a lot of good and necessary changes in colleagues, and in me.'

Before WAVE could apply for a second funding grant, the biologists had to secure local ministers' approval of the country-level plans for responding to the threat of emerging cassava diseases. This was no small challenge: pulling together diverse officials from each country to craft a consensus that all their governments would approve. But they succeeded and are now implementing a prototype system in Nigeria. Pita and Kahn effervesce in their enthusiasm for the work, but also for their newfound confidence in tackling challenges that had initially frightened them as much as any military battle. Neither doubts that the two weeks they spent with Olivier and his team changed and enhanced the prospects for WAVE, for the people of East and West Africa, and it's striking how keenly they both retain the feeling and the facts of their experience.

You could argue that this is all a tad utilitarian: Shakespeare didn't write his plays just to make future scientists or organizational leadership teams more effective. Of course not (although he was, of course, fantastically canny at observing how the political world works). But that Olivier's programme is so far removed from the conventional experience of work reflects just how desiccated and brittle our working lives have become, its jargon stripped of poetry, and its sense of purpose too often expressed through cash rewards. Reinvigorating the humanity intrinsic to the problems

Pita and Kahn confronted wasn't just about making them better at their jobs; it was about restoring their capacity to energize themselves and those around them.

At UCL, with more than 16,000 staff and over 50,000 students from 150 countries and a multibillion-pound budget, provost Michael Spence is not very different from anyone leading a complex organization in times of great uncertainty. Referencing the American legal philosopher Ronald Dworkin, Spence describes a university as 'a theatre for the exercise of the independence of the mind', a place of constant search for new ideas, and where old or inferior ones can be debunked. His job is not to know all the answers, but to curate the appropriate debates. Early in his tenure, he also called on Olivier's programme for his senior leadership team. The safer place of the play enabled conversation, about patterns of behaviour and engagement, that they would never have had otherwise.

'I have a team', he said, 'whose characteristic is both a strength and a weakness, which is making decision by intuition and we need people who are very analytically driven. So each needs the foil for the other.'

Speaking of his own background – his first degree in English and Italian – he said, 'I think a degree in language and literature developed a capacity to understand that there's more than one way to see a problem. If you spend a lot of time in fiction, you learn to think about "what is the interior monologue with the person with whom I'm engaging?" The discipline of a background like this is that it forces you to encounter monologues different from your own. I think it's a tendency of humanities training always to be thinking: it could be another way.'

'We have students protesting about Israel/Palestine and demanding divestments. We had huge income issues last year, we still have some income issues this year. We have huge building projects going and the builder has gone bust. We are revising our disciplinary processes and the union is in chaos. So when I go into my meeting this afternoon, I expect the people I work with to test the ideas we have for dealing with each situation.'

* * *

Drama lets us watch others as a way of seeing both them and ourselves. But it can go further than that. After graduating, Dan Barnard and Rachel Briscoe worked in theatre but felt constrained and frustrated by its conventions, and particularly by the passive role of the audience. They were more drawn to exploring how we might react, and interact, if placed inside imagined situations in real time. So they started to play in a different way: creating situations where audience members were the protagonists – everyone watching and interacting with everyone else. In a 2015 piece, *Invisible Treasure*, they explored ideas of complicity and agency inside invisible systems (like the internet, financial markets, the power grid) by creating an interactive digital playspace in which the spectators were given clues about the temporary society they inhabited. Over the period of the 'show' its rules became increasingly repressive. As visitors figured out how the place functioned, how would they respond – with complicity, with agency, with solidarity, or with fracture? The audience were the performers, making choices together, responding to shifting power dynamics and defining for themselves the boundaries of acceptable behaviour. It was a little like being inside a computer game, with the crucial differences that physical space and the other people were all real and the decision making was driven by interactions within the group. 'We're really interested', Briscoe says, 'in how we can make immersive experiences where the participants' primary relationship is with each other, rather than with us or with "the artwork".'

The show used a lot of technology, but that wasn't its point. They'd found a sweet spot that has fuelled their work ever since, using interactive technology and detailed real-world scenarios to explore areas of uncertainty: emergencies, justice, climate change. Working at the intersection of theatre and social science, Briscoe and Barnard could learn, but so would their participants; they wanted people to experience the world, not just consume it. Wandering through this unexplored territory, they were 'planting questions and growing answers'.[27]

In 2019, their SHUTDOWN project simulated a seven-day power outage in the UK. This wasn't entertainment but a highly pragmatic exploration: knowing that a National Grid outage could take up to a week to restore, the Cabinet Office could not predict how people would behave. Surveys would be of questionable value; since few of us have ever lived through a week-long power outage, we don't really know how we'd respond. SHUTDOWN was an imaginative response to the quantum problem posed by large numbers that don't reliably illuminate individual variability.

Working with neuroscientist Kris De Meyer, Briscoe and Barnard had hoped to stage a real and prolonged blackout; that proved too difficult and expensive. So they developed a story about five citizens caught in the emergency. To create an experience as real as possible, a storyline was created using video testimony (played by actors) interspersed with dramatized national emergency broadcasts, official communications and documentary footage. In effect, it had all the ingredients of a documentary that might have been made after the event, with the difference that, at each critical stage, it could be stopped and choices made.

As the drama unfolded, participants were asked specific questions about each character's behaviour and about the preparation and readiness of government departments. How acceptable was it that one of the characters disobeyed instructions not to stockpile water in their bathtubs? If they travelled despite official guidance to stay home? A number of participants realized that they themselves would disobey in order to be with vulnerable family members; on the other hand, many would follow advice not to go to A&E to charge their mobile phones. Almost everyone considered that raiding supermarkets would be legitimate, prompting the suggestion that it might be best for stores to keep their doors open. The project also demonstrated that people would work together, but that levels of trust and social cohesion would vary. Those who remembered blackouts from the 1970s showed more resilience, as did those who had experience of extreme weather events. Most illuminating of all were the rich ideas and initiatives that participants came up with, suggestions that could help local and national policy makers prepare for an event that remains possible but unpredictable.[28]

It's hard to read about this simulation without wishing it had been done for pandemic planning – not because SHUTDOWN produced rock-solid plans, but because it revealed the contours of the challenge, weaving a richly textured picture of the spectrum of responses. The scenario didn't eliminate uncertainty but it did identify potential pragmatic courses of action. It also made very clear how far you can't treat the public as one consistent group, either of lawbreakers or compliant citizens. That the conclusions derived from very diverse audiences provided a cross section of possible responses. Because each participant's judgements remained confidential, this reduced the risk of groupthink because none of the participants knew how others replied. That made the data a more trustworthy guide, a more insightful basis for preparation.

Now known as Fast Familiar, the team's more recent project, The Strategy Room, addresses climate change: how can local authorities gauge which policies would gain traction within their communities and which would be rejected? What initiatives would be uncontentious – but possibly ineffective? Which would be too forceful for a democracy? Beyond the crisis itself, the great tragedy of climate change has been the epic communications failure to enable policy makers, businesses and citizens to craft coherent, effective adaptation. Fear doesn't force behaviour change, and the brittle language of incentives doesn't come close to what's needed to avoid food shortages, mass migration, economic and social havoc. It's become tragically clear that technical explanations of the science are utterly inadequate to drive change, so the urgent need to design deeper, more human strategies has been obvious, but stalled, for years. Nobody knows what will work, so instead of being led by ideology and assumptions, why not play it through – and see?

Fast Familiar approaches this problem not as an argument or a debate, but as a collective imagining of possible futures. Again, using scripted personal testimonies, participants respond confidentially about their priorities and concerns. Because information comes to them through characters (it's a human problem), nobody is harangued or lectured; attendees are simply given the opportunity to experience what could happen. Might using the techniques of drama to simulate what could happen, how that might feel, bring the topic to life and help policy makers and citizens better appreciate what they could do right now?[29]

Climate change is, of course, awash with uncertainties. We know that it is real – in this project just one participant out of 639 challenged the facts. But people feel paralysed by uncertainty, not knowing *exactly* what, *exactly* when, where or how we will reach tipping points. Governments are similarly confused, their fear of going too far, too fast, paralysing them. That, coupled with the complexity of climate itself, leaves people feeling hopeless, full of grief, anger and an overwhelming sense of peril. It also leaves a vacuum, all too easily filled by vested interests and propagandists, threatening to leave democracies undefended and ineffective.

What the Fast Familiar project provided was a series of scenarios that described how particular climate policies on, say, travel might change an individual's life. How would travel restrictions impact an electric wheelchair user, urban or rural inhabitants? Opinions were polled individually (to avoid groupthink) followed by a facilitated group discussion that explored alternatives and trade-offs. This was all very real, practical and personal, and offered a deep insight into how the future lived experience of different individuals might reconcile often contradictory values, their tolerance for change and their deep concerns about fairness. With a process for civil discussion, the human dynamics that Fast Familiar designed and tested provided local authorities with a greater understanding of social behaviours and a richer assortment of validated possibilities.

Fast Familiar puts participants, as Briscoe says, 'in the story, not in the stalls'. Because the exercise was done collectively, it made them more alert to the impact of their decisions on others, something surveys can never capture. It's no wonder participants were left excited, stimulated by the thoughts and possibilities the experience had provoked. Learning how other people see things can be galvanizing, inspiring; it opens up alternative vistas in a lively, human and safe way. By providing a context in which participants could rehearse real lives in a well-described and specific way, they gave the groups an experience of the unknown. Just as *Henry V* had aroused deep imaginative comparison and exploration in the minds of scientists, Fast Familiar's theatre gave a cross section of citizens an opportunity to explore themselves and their community in all their complexity, and it developed an ecosystem of options for decision makers. The exercise also demonstrated that, brought together to consider a difficult, contentious subject, all these different people could communicate.

Polarization was not inevitable. People could imagine embracing the give and take that the crisis will demand.

The Fast Familiar team, Briscoe, Barnard and computational artist Joe McAlister have gone on to work with other kinds of organizations grappling with contentious places and ideas: hospitals, juries, the legacies of colonialism. But a programme as inventive and original as theirs is inevitably difficult to describe and hard to sell to institutions afraid to experiment. That's one reason Briscoe and her colleagues are so fastidious about collecting data all the way along: to demonstrate clearly how the process works, where and how changes occur in people, and how the participants explain them. It's a highly thoughtful, well-documented use of technology, drama and information. But it's difficult and time-consuming to identify clients brave enough, sufficiently dissatisfied with the status quo, to try something so new and complex. When we met, Briscoe and Barnard had just had their first child. How did they deal with their own uncertainty?

'Being freelance is less bad than I thought it would be', Briscoe shrugged. 'We have a margin of security, savings and somewhere to live. I think it's also a lack of shame: if it all goes wrong, somebody will employ me to do something; I worked in a restaurant for five years!'

'But now it seems to me like there are two types of uncertainty. The first is where the ball is in your court and you have control over what happens next. So most of the things we've talked about – complex projects, working with partners, negotiating an existence where there is no long-term stability or accepted plan – in those situations, you have a high degree of control over what happens next. This sounds counter-intuitive but, because there isn't an accepted roadmap, no one expects you to follow it and you don't know what's going to happen. What you do have is autonomy over each choice you make. There isn't a script, so you can write it as you go.'

She felt less comfort with the second type of uncertainty: when her newborn baby daughter was ill, she had so little expertise, autonomy or control. But in the wider uncertainty of life, the team is inventing ways to imagine uncertain futures, to elucidate its contours and its choices, to identify the spaces in which action and agency have impact, where we need not be helpless or passive. In that respect, Fast Familiar has a deep democratic undertow: let's see what we're made of. Like all the artists in this book, the uncertainty that Briscoe and her colleagues confront is offset by the rewards that action brings, new discoveries and inventions along the way. It's a far richer, more human and more complex approach to change than the force-fitted tyranny of behaviourism. It feels more fruitful and effective than the wilfully brutal so-called transformation programmes foisted by consultants on employees as if those were just machines in need of re-engineering. And instead of imposing more jargon and bureaucracy, the process leaves behind experience and memories that grow and proliferate in all walks of life for years to come.

The dawning recognition that the future demands far more of us than efficiency, technology, metrics, rewards and sanctions is encouraging, a weak signal acknowledging that we are more, and can offer more, than a mechanical model of life, however glitzy. That art can give people hope, a sense of belonging, that it can reconnect us to each other beautifully, expanding all the gifts and talents we bring to an uncertain future. So I'm heartened, not surprised, each time I find organizations turning to the arts to explore, energize and revive the creative human capacity in their people.

At Oxford Saïd Business School, an executive programme works with Rob Poynton, an improvisation artist who draws a direct line from his art to the uncertainties that organizational leaders face daily. Improv artists don't start with nothing; like Lucy McLauchlan, their minds are always full of possible openings, ready when needed. When you don't know what to do, try something. You might not have a plan, but you can come prepared.

A group of former CEOs being taught how to draw with pastels is, for some, a test; for others, a contest. But for most, it is a lesson in observation, in patience, in considering the connection between seeing and doing.

A poetry workshop for executives revealed new ways of thinking, listening to what was really going on in their minds. Much to my surprise, they were eager to read their poems out loud, and the following day, several decided to make poetry routine, not an exception. Why? It made them feel alive. And it helped them to think, the one thing they're paid for but rarely have time to do.

In Portugal, medical students study poetry for similar reasons, learning to be less transactional, not to see each patient as just a data point or a problem that needs solving. Poetry succinctly captures complexity; the more carefully you read, the more you see, something true of every patient they will meet. It's helpful that many doctors (William Carlos Williams, John Keats, Friedrich Schiller, Dannie Abse, Miroslav Holub) have also been poets, so there's plenty of material that aspiring doctors can relate to, and the connection between surgery and rewriting is an easy one to make.

When Yale School of Medicine found that their students were poor diagnosticians, they could have just added more diagnosis modules. Instead, they collaborated with the Yale Center for British Art, which offered the aspiring doctors sessions in which they looked at works in the collection and had to describe them. They could not simply say that the portrait showed a depressed person, but had to specify the features that led them to their conclusions. Where before students had looked for what they expected to see, now they searched in detail to find how observations connected, what they might mean, and what else might be going on. This group's scores increased by 25 per cent compared to a control group learning in a lecture theatre. Subsequent courses also showed that trainee doctors learn to see better if they draw. Natural science students typically don't have much tolerance for uncertainty – they want answers – so learning to slow down and observe without an agenda, to ask questions of themselves, not just of patients, is critical.[30]

The close viewing of art inculcates in clinicians the appreciation that more than one interpretation of an image may exist. As medical schools and institutions (the National Academies of Sciences, Engineering, and Medicine and the World Health Organization) have opened their minds to the value of the arts and humanities, they keep finding that these improve a broad range of clinical capabilities: critical thinking, tolerance of ambiguity and empathy. Body painting turns out to be a good way to teach anatomy. And Visual Thinking Strategies (VTS) are widely used to improve observation and interpretation skills, useful to detectives at crime scenes as well as to diagnosticians.[31]

At UCL, sitting in Michael Spence's office, just across the street from one of London's biggest hospitals, it was impossible not to notice the many intriguing paintings on the wall. We started to look at one of them, *The Tragedians*, painted by David Bomberg, which featured three panels. In the middle was a single person against a golden background; darker panels either side contained two people. Spence referred to them as his 'grumpy old men'. But as we looked more carefully, it wasn't clear that they were all men; the central figure seemed (to me at least) to be female. Were they grumpy – or just contemplative? What did the golden background mean? Later, Spence was delighted to learn that Bomberg had been expelled from the Slade School of Fine Art because of the radicalism of his approach. The more we looked, the more we saw. An interview had turned into a conversation.

These examples – and there are many more – sound fun, and why shouldn't they be? Implicitly the experiments that integrate art into all walks of life acknowledge the poverty of the behaviourist, efficient and transactional mindsets that have beguiled policy makers for generations. The ruthless pursuit of bigger, faster and cheaper, the binary obsession that defines everyone and everything either as a problem or a solution, an allergy to the ambiguous and ambivalent, has left us anxious, unimaginative, uncritical, unwilling or incapable of seeing or responding to the complexity of life in all its colour, variety, perspectives and depth.

It's tempting – and common – to dismiss all this as so much art nonsense, to argue that instead of digging into all this complexity, subtlety and uncertainty we should just embrace the promise of artificial intelligence and leave it to technology to figure out what we can't. But there are immense difficulties with the substitution of our native intelligence with AI. Many have been recognized for years: incomplete, error-strewn data sets, biased models, dependence on historic data, subjective and rigid definitions of reward or success, the fact that not all problems are solved by trial and error, and that many brilliant breakthroughs derive from apparently irrelevant disciplines. A deeper fundamental issue is legitimacy. A good decision must satisfy many conditions, not least among which is that it can be explained, so that even those who may not like the decision can live with it. This does not apply to automatically generated decisions reached in ways nobody knows or comprehends. Moreover, when we outsource to technology the skills and tasks we prefer not to do, we lose the ability to do those tasks ourselves. Making ourselves dependent on machines to make decisions that we have lost the ability to take for ourselves doesn't diminish but amplifies risk, fragility and uncertainty.

The ensuing binary argument – regulate, or the technology will kill us *vs* any delay will destroy us – is typically bullying and simplistic. AI doesn't make our problems disappear; its challenge simply makes more evident the urgent need for cross-cultural understanding. If it is possible to develop the safety and legitimacy that its proponents promise, then that will require deep, complex collaboration across multiple disciplines. We know by now that all discoveries and innovation present unexpected consequences, which economists call perverse outcomes and physicians call side effects. To expect this new technology to be any different is either naive, negligent or criminal. It will be essential to test AI and its applications, as we already do for drugs: to see who, and where, and in what circumstances it causes harm.

At Stuart Russell's AI lab at Berkeley, historians, anthropologists, philosophers, sociologists and artists have to work together if they are to have any understanding of the benefits and risks of new technology. It is very striking the degree to which management and leadership scholars are not at this table; notable, too, that Russell's practice is not widely emulated in competitive, commercial tech businesses. But convening, managing and deriving pragmatic conclusions from such polyglot groups demands the complex and subtle understanding that the biologists learned from *Henry V*. Noticing, imagining, exploring the space between perspectives, living with paradoxes: these will always be critical to such conversations, especially if the decisions that emerge from them are to have any legitimacy; without that, just binary thinking and rage.

The benefit of art is not reserved for the artist alone (most people who study or enjoy the arts don't go on to become artists), but is broadly diffused, enabling us to see more, identify a wider range of responses and possibilities, to offer a richer array of perspectives and choices for ourselves and all those around us. If we are to respond creatively to discontinuous change, we need to develop in ourselves and in rising generations a greater capacity to imagine, to invent and experiment in ways that are legitimate and humane. Companies routinely struggle with this – but artists do it ceaselessly. Fierce pragmatists, they are accustomed to, often inspired by, working under extreme constraints. Like Henry V, the WAVE scientists and UCL leadership team, we can learn the fine art of reflection, sense making, the capacity to integrate personal expertise with the knowledge of others, which is the essential heart of leadership.

Art alone won't solve everything and doesn't replace the need for science, for law, for technology: that would be another false binary. The traditional need for deep knowledge of a discipline is as fundamental as ever; knowing what it is to understand something deeply is to discern the difference between knowledge and opinion. What the arts contribute is a greater capacity for inventiveness, discovery, humanity, courage and resilience. The art critic Robert Hughes argued that the greater the artist, the greater the doubt. The same might, and should, be said of anyone trying to do something new that matters: to keep looking for disconfirmation, early signs of surprise while remaining deeply aware of the urgency of now.

Why are these skills so essential to leadership? Because observation, communication and noticing are fundamental to being able to galvanize groups of people to tackle threats and surprises, whether Henry V becoming king, scientists negotiating to keep crops alive or citizens surviving power outages. But the world in which people blindly obey impersonal, inhumane decisions made by nobody is the Skinnerian daydream in which all we do in our lives is turn up and follow incentives.

When Andy Haldane was chief economist at the Bank of England, he often reflected on how common it is, following a crisis, to become risk-averse, timid, too traumatized by the past to make courageous decisions about the future. But that is to fail to rise to the challenge of recovery and reinvention.

'We are at a juncture where we have to refresh and rethink', Andy Haldane argues now. Having ridden the tumult of the

Global Financial Crisis, he doesn't believe anything since has got simpler. We need more of who we are, not less.

'We can't just double down on the old stuff. It makes our thinking rigid and blinds us to the very problems that got us where we are now. And tech won't answer all these problems. It's useful in assimilating facts in a press-the-button way, but it mustn't be mistaken for judgement. Judgements that really matter aren't refinable in that way; they need an overlay of imagination and intuition. Most of the mistakes in my career have been when I've ignored that and gone with the prevailing narrative, but it's always, always will be, a mistake not to think for yourself.'

CHRISTINE VACHON

The film producer Christine Vachon is getting ready to go to Mexico where her new film, directed by Todd Haynes, is beginning shooting.

'This is always the worst part, when you're just pulling all the pieces together, and just when you think it's all together and you can relax, somebody pulls out a string and the whole thing collapses again, and you have to put it back together. In some ways I'm more effective sitting in New York in my office than I will be in Guadalajara with shitty Wi-Fi and not able to speak the language, and it's ridiculous that I never was able to learn any Spanish. ...'

Vachon's films have primarily been independents made on small budgets.

'My first film was a film called *Poison* (1991). One of the many things that revealed itself to me as we took it out into the world to the Sundance Film Festival, and it won the Grand Jury Prize, was that there was a pretty substantial audience that really wanted to see itself represented and would pay to do so. And if you made it for the right amount of money, it would make its money back. And that was a pretty extraordinary thing to figure out.'

The producer of over 60 films, she runs Killer Films with her business partner, Pamela Koffler.

'At Killer Films ... we really kind of go after what we like. And that tends to be things that have something to say. Something to say now – or in a year or two because that's how long it can take to reach people. And, underserved audiences, tales that aren't usually told, other points of view that nobody's noticed.'

'You can't really reverse engineer success. You can't say: these movies were successful, so we're going to take these elements ... what matters is the reality of what you just see with your own eyes. I just go for the stories that are meaningful to me.'

Indie films have always been challenging, but ever since the 1980s the industry has been going through some form of disruption.

'The demise of the kind of movies I make has been predicted constantly! The big disruptions in my career – starting to shoot on video, or digital instead of film, cable, then VHS, DVDs, home rental, streamers – all of those things were giant disruptors. But I try to revel in the changes, in the pivots. One of the reasons Killer has stayed around so long is because we really do adapt.'

And more than a few of her films have turned out to be far ahead of their time.

'Our films have long lives and a good example is *Safe* (1995), which nobody saw when it came out. But then people discovered it as time went on – and it's still a movie people go back to. People say it still feels new. So one of the great, great things about being able to see films in so many different formats now is that they don't disappear the way they used to.'

In 1996, *The New York Times* calls Vachon the 'godmother of the politically committed film'.

'Making a movie like *Boys Don't Cry* is a political act, no matter how you spin it. It just is. We were trying to say that trans people were people – but let the movie speak for itself. You could say the same thing about a movie like *Beatrix at Dinner*, which I also call the *White Lotus* proof-of-concept film! *Past Lives*, people will talk to me about it because it meant so much to them as an immigrant. They felt that it captured something about their experience that they had never seen before.'

Does art change anything?

'I think it changes everything. Otherwise we wouldn't keep doing it.'

5

Kill all the poets: art and politics

> The function of art is to do more than tell it like it
> is — it's to imagine what is possible.
>
> bell hooks[1]

Derry. Londonderry. The second largest town in Northern
Ireland, mostly ignored by tourists. If you mention it, the
first thing people will ask is why it has two names. But still,
most people call it Derry.

On a cold, wet Sunday morning, the town seems tired from
the night before, with just a few women walking and families
driving to church. Everyone says 'hello', although they don't
know you. I'm doubtful the Guildhall will be open so I am
surprised when it is — and warm too. Like many such Victorian
public buildings, it looks and feels like a church, with its tall
tower, Gothic windows and noisy, tiled floors. The layout isn't
obvious, but after consoling a hungover man for his error in
mistaking the Ladies for the Gents, I find the room that is the
museum. It tells the city's rocky history, from the Elizabethan
plantation to the Troubles. A sign brings us up to date.

> 1972: The Guildhall is bombed by the IRA. It is
> refurbished, opening again in 1978.
> 1980: World premiere at the Guildhall of the first
> production by the Field Day Theatre Company.
> 2010: The conclusion of the Saville Inquiry into the
> events of Bloody Sunday.

Sandwiched between two records of violence, a new theatre company founded by the playwright Brian Friel and the actor Stephen Rea appears as an equivalent event.

'I wanted to go to Derry', Rea told me. 'I wanted to go to where theatre wasn't. They didn't have *anything* in Derry. ...'

In 1980, Rea's career was largely in London theatre and Friel's was all over the world – Dublin, London, New York. But he came from Derry, and an earlier play, *Freedom of the City*, was set right there, in a thinly disguised Guildhall during Bloody Sunday. When Rea approached him about touring a new play, both men agreed that it should not just be for an urban elite, but they should seek out rural audiences usually ignored by commercial theatre. They also leaned towards Irish poet Patrick Kavanagh's notion of parochialism.

'Apart from Synge' Friel said at the time, 'all our dramatists have pitched their voice for English acceptance and recognition. ... I think that for the first time, that is stopping, that there is some kind of confidence, some kind of coming together of Irish dramatists who have no interest in the English stage. We are talking to ourselves as we must. ...'[2]

Field Day's debut would be *Translations*, a play about (among other things) the naming of places. Its world premiere would be in Derry; for a city accustomed to being in the news only when tragedy and violence erupted, the pair's decision was deliberate, provocative and difficult. To call the project uncertain would be an understatement. For one thing, there was no theatre in Derry. Using the Guildhall building was contentious – a symbol of unionism in the midst of a predominantly nationalist population. But it was the biggest space in town, and the lure of a Friel premiere was catalytic; the sheer unexpected boldness of the idea drew people to it. So, when the City Council offered Field Day the building's auditorium, together with a promise of lighting and a new stage, and the British government's instant response was to deny any new money for it, the Council became determined to find the necessary funds themselves.

'Everything was essentially political', Rea remembers. 'We lived in a sectarian society, a hideously sectarian society and all our discussions were about that.'

The creation of Field Day proved a startlingly creative response to the profound uncertainties that had beset Northern Ireland for centuries. Instead of yielding to passivity or paralysis, Rea and Friel took action – but nobody knew what the outcome would be. Neither was a producer or director, and they had no grand plan or strategy (for success or failure), just an instinctive drive not to be bystanders but to do something in the face of horror and tragedy.

'When we started Field Day' Rea remembers, 'it was a certain shambles, because there was no theatre infrastructure in Derry, no stage carpenters, no costumes. But that meant everyone helped us, they came from all over to pitch in with costumes and lighting boards. It was almost our amateurishness – I was an actor, Friel was a writer – that drew them in. There was never any money. We just did it. We used to call ourselves Black and Decker because we were so tough. It was sublime really.'

And so, for once in Derry there was good news. That Friel's new play would premiere in a town formerly known only for division, anger and disappointment was unimaginable; it meant something, even if nobody could agree what. That a playwright as prestigious as Friel, and an actor as celebrated as Rea, would commit so much of their time and energy to a city that felt neglected and abused was exceptional and public interest intense.

As cast members visited local schools and journalists competed to cover every detail of the production, the play sold out fast. On opening night, the Guildhall was still barricaded against terrorist attacks, scaffolding covering earlier bomb damage, but the place was packed. For what felt like the first time in centuries, something new and creative was happening in Derry: 'A unique occasion, with loyalists and nationalist, Unionist and SDLP, Northerners and Southerners, laying aside their differences to join together in applauding a play by a fellow Derryman',[3] wrote the *Irish Press* about a premiere whose atmosphere was so dramatic – 'an electric love affair' – that the review of the play itself had to wait for the next day. The production could have run for months but a tour was already set up, travelling to small towns and villages just like the ones where the play is set.

'It was so thrilling to go round the country and people came out everywhere', Rea recalls. 'In Enniskillen, the church hall, people came out because we had come to them. They'd come home from the fields, have their tea and come out again, bringing their chairs with them. There was never enough room! It was after a day's work but people weren't tired. A man came up to me and said he'd never been in theatre before, but he got it. We got incredible loyalty from those people.'

Reviews then and since acclaimed *Translations* as a great and subtle play about language, colonial occupation and identity. Its story revolves around the arrival in the 1830s of British cartographers mapping the region and replacing Gaelic names with Anglicized versions as they went. The local hedge school, teaching Greek and Latin, is to be closed down, replaced by a new national education system where English is compulsory. The place feels likes it is being invaded, but Friel eschews binary stereotypes. The romantic British lieutenant Yolland isn't a monster; he worries that removing Gaelic names will undermine Irish culture, while a young local woman, Maire, is neither servile nor furious; she yearns for the language of America. Surveyors and locals can't speak the same language; misunderstanding is rife, sometimes comic, more often threatening, as likely to provoke conflict as resolve it. Yet even without a shared language, Maire and Yolland communicate their love for one another. Ever since that first opening night in Derry, *Translations* has been acclaimed for its profound exploration of the political power of language: to constrain ideas but also to defy force.

Did that make it a political play? Everything about its opening was freighted with meaning, but even Friel wasn't sure. Before it opened, he worried in his diary, 'Are the characters only mouthpieces. ... Is the play only an ideas play?', while years later he insisted that 'the play has to do with language and only language', arguing, 'The problem with the Northern situation is how you can tiptoe through the minefields of language when language has become so politicized.'[4]

Rea had, and has, no such doubts about the play or about founding a theatre company in the heart of the Troubles.

'We were opening people's minds', he insists. 'People in Belfast and Dublin, they weren't facing the issues. But because Friel had written this play, it made us face the issues. It reawakened people to their history. People knew it meant something. They were worn out with the violence and we made people take Irish culture seriously. People knew it meant something.'

If Friel was uncertain about his play, nobody had any doubts about the politics of the Field Day project. The arts had long been a crucible for political ideas and debate in Ireland. Its history and revolution were illuminated and inflamed by poetry, rhetoric, theatre and music. The historian Roy Foster points out how many aspects of the revolutionary period were, in themselves, both political and theatrical: funerals, demonstrations, pageants and travelling *tableaux vivants* that crossed the country, visiting neglected communities, towns and villages in just the same way that *Translations* did now.[5] W.B. Yeats might be said to have been both a dramatist and protagonist in the story of the Republic's birth, and in his creation of the Abbey Theatre with the specific intention 'to bring upon the stage the deeper emotions of Ireland'.[6] It was there that plays were met with riots, whether they ignored political issues – John Millington Synge's *Playboy of the Western World* – or addressed them head-on – Seán O'Casey's *The Plough and the Stars*. However ambivalent Friel might have felt about the tenor of his play, it was met by an audience fully expecting to encounter political ideas.

Field Day went on to produce more than theatre. For 10 years, a collective flourished, attracting some of the finest writers in English to their project: Seamus Heaney, Seamus Deane, Tom Paulin, Derek Mahon, Stewart Parker, Thomas Kilroy. None of these men (and they were all men) lacked strong political opinions, and the publishing arm of Field Day was renowned for the depth and articulacy of its annual review of Irish cultural and political life and for its pamphlets. In the second of these, *An Open Letter*, Heaney's epistolary poem abandons ambivalence ('Your Prince of Denmark Hesitation') in favour of a clear definition of his national identity:

> Don't be surprised
> If I demur, for, be advised
> My passport's green.
> No glass of ours was ever raised
> To toast *The Queen*.[7]

Deane, whom Rea describes as 'the greatest intellect the country ever had', edited the landmark five-volume *Field Day Anthology of Irish Writing* while also writing extensive programme notes for the company's annual theatre production.

'It was great', Rea says, 'to be able to take Deane out of the academy into direct address with ordinary people. He wrote screeds for the programmes and people were reading that. He was politicizing the performances in the best sense.'

Not every play was explicitly political, although Rea says that the choice of *Antigone* definitely was. So, too, was the commitment to choosing plays that looked far beyond Northern Ireland. Producing work by Athol Fugard, Chekhov, Sophocles and Molière, with translations by Heaney, Friel, Paulin and Mahon, the collective sought to connect Northern Irish audiences with a bigger, wider world of ideas and perspectives. In the same way that Field Day's rural tours owed something to traditional Irish travelling players, its policy of mounting European classics echoed efforts made by the art dealer and collector Hugh Lane to introduce Irish audiences to contemporary European painting, especially French impressionists. From 1904 until his death in 1915, Lane had campaigned for the establishment of a modern art gallery, seeking to broaden and update the Republic's sense of itself, to develop an identity as rich and varied as any European nation. So, too, the range and quality of Field Day's theatre explicitly aimed to rescue a beleaguered, violent, economically and psychically depressed province from the provincialism in which it had been mired.

In its wake followed a rich proliferation of new young theatre companies – Rough Magic, Red Kettle, Charabanc – that continued to establish Irish theatre as a force to be reckoned with: cosmopolitan, sophisticated, witty and smart. They weren't imitators and their founders were younger, with less experience and less authority than the founders of Field Day.

'They were all incredibly august! I mean, you're talking about the top bananas! We didn't have that', Lynne Parker says. She founded the Dublin-based theatre company Rough Magic in 1984. 'We were just very bumptious, all of us, and absolutely unafraid. The circumstances in Ireland were as bleak as you can imagine – hunger strikes and a deep, deep recession, like nothing we know now. But you had minimal rent to pay so it was possible to live. Uncertainty was almost beneficial because we didn't have any targets to reach; we were just shooting for the moon, making stuff and learning as we went along.'

Rough Magic was just as determined to broaden the kind of theatre done in Ireland, producing local and international playwrights. In doing so, the company challenged the notion of an Irish identity that was rural and backward looking. In their embrace of new writing, and fresh interpretations of classic writers like William Wycherley, Friedrich Schiller and Bertolt Brecht, they seek, in their own way, to look towards a theatre still firmly based in language and storytelling but focused on the present and the future. What Parker and her contemporaries, and Field Day, all had going for them, she says, was their confidence that the making of art was a serious and powerful activity.

'It feels to me as if the Irish have always taken the theatre, arts, language very, very seriously. There's a fundamental cultural belief here that art matters, that you have to show the truth. Art is a reflection, it is the mirror. And it's the job of the artist to unflinchingly tell the truth and to be honest. And as a consequence that may give it a capacity to influence popular thinking here in a way that's tougher in other places.'

In his Oxford Lectures on poetry, *The Redress of Poetry*, Heaney describes a poem as a response to reality, a 'glimpsed alternative' that sets up contradictions with our own experience. What does the poet see that you don't? How do I think, feel about the differences between us? That internal conversation, between you and it, is the heart of the matter. All art is a form of collaboration – those 'co-conspirators' – creating a dialogue that may be conscious or unconscious, intimate or internalized. It doesn't aim to eliminate uncertainty, but to illuminate its possibilities.

Of course, this isn't unique to poetry. Paintings present a view of reality that is not yours, inviting you to consider all that lies between the two of you. Even points of coincidence involve a fresh recognition: yes, that is *just* how it is! Drama and narrative depend on conflict, the collision between points of view; often the alternative is not so much glimpsed as explored. Even at its most oblique or uncertain, the contrast between lives on stage and our lives offstage is endemic. Music paints an emotional landscape to which we may or may not relate; at its best, it does both. So the experience of art carries within it at least a hint of change and a rejection of inevitability.

To us, now, it might not look like the classics carry any hint of the times that produced them. To us today, they often feel timeless, eternal. But Ancient Greek theatre wasn't conceived in some kind of white marble Athenian bubble; it was performed before audiences alert to war. Aristophanes' comedy *Lysistrata* can be seen as just a ribald feminist satire, in which women gain power by denying men sexual favours. But written at the time of the Peloponnesian War, Aristophanes' audience would have been highly attuned to a live political argument around the male propensity for violence. Similarly Aeschylus' *The Persians* is about the dangers of military overreach; *Seven against Thebes* shows protagonists Polyneices and Eteocles winning only enough territory for their graves. Sophocles' *Philoctetes* is a brutal, incisive exposé of the ethical destruction wrought in men who have spent years on the battlefield. Having served as a general in the Samian War, Sophocles knew its realities, the destructive tensions between obedience, loyalty and honesty. So when Field Day commissioned Heaney to adapt the play, it needed very little adjustment to connect ancient Greece in 409 BC to Derry audiences in 1990:

> Heroes. Victims. Gods and human beings.
> All throwing shapes, every one of them
> Convinced he's in the right, all of them glad
> To repeat themselves and their every last mistake.

But Heaney added a new Chorus at the end:

> Suspect too much sweet talk
> But never close your mind.
> It was a fortunate wind
> That blew me here. I leave
> Half-ready to believe
> That a crippled trust might walk
>
> And the half-true rhyme is love.[8]

Today, Rea's claims for Field Day are modest, but far from trivial. He says, 'it gave people a new way to think and feel about what they were living through. It made movement possible.' Deane thought that 'it made a contribution towards the achievement of the peaceful non-sectarian society that emerged in Ireland somewhere in the next century.'

We have no valid theories of change and we can't do the experiment: take all the arts out of Irish history and see what we get. Political art emerges from within a context, and that setting means that its audiences bring much more to it than the work alone: hopes, disappointments, grudges and dreams. You could see this as an extreme form of public collaboration: between the work, its audiences and the lived experience of the time and place – a rich brew no document or recording can measure. Which means that the impact of Field Day can never be considered in isolation from the times that gave rise to it.

But you can look back at the period between the Troubles and the Good Friday Agreement and at the exceptional production of artistic work during that period, and assess where it tends. Look, for instance, at the end of *Translations*, which does not end with slaughter, a call to arms or a stand-off, but with an ambiguous shared tension around fear and loss. There are no villains or angels in the plays that Field Day produced; instead, there's a vast exploration that encourages audiences, together, to imagine being those people at that time in those situations – what would we feel? What choices would we make? That's a very long way from sectarian binaries.

Educating the imagination is how Mahon believed that poetry allows us to see beyond our own circumscribed lives.[9] It could be said of all the arts, that in the depths of violence, occupation, a dismal social and economic life, such work by all these theatre companies provided alternative views of life but could not, alone, forge peace. Of course, more, far more, was needed, is needed. But what art can be said plausibly to have contributed to 20th-century Irish history was a willingness, a capacity to reimagine, a broadening of outlook and a softening of hearts that made peace thinkable.

Archaeologists may have defined art as something with no pragmatic utility, but that is not to say that it does nothing. Art creates the conditions in which people can feel and consider their circumstances in ways that are complex and subtle. It is distinct from propaganda that simplifies and urges us to take action without reflection or feeling. Art does not purport to be a solution to a problem; it doesn't exist within that efficient framing of life. It is a means of addressing uncertainty by exploring, not running away from it. Artists seek, find and query alternatives – that's the work they do daily – confident of finding them if they have the patience to search. While propaganda lives off false promises of certainty and inevitability, that isn't the artist's game; the possibility of change, a refusal to see the world only as it appears in the moment, is. At its quietest, art poses questions; at its loudest, it is defiant. That it does this both in public and in private is what makes it potent, but also dangerous.

It is often said that when the poet Edmund Spenser went to Ireland to help settle the Munster plantation for Elizabeth I, he advised her that if the country were truly to be settled and its native language expunged, she would need first to kill all the poets, such was their power and authority in the land. A highly esteemed poet himself, it is unclear whether or not he believed this achievable or desirable. What is certain is that throughout history, governments and institutions have feared artists because they make people think, feel, question and care, because art brings people together and creates conditions in which they can reach out to each other and, in doing so, make themselves more powerful. In its uncompromising capacity to synthesize heart and mind, personal reflection with political action, even at its darkest, political art whispers: you are not alone in thinking it doesn't have to be this way.

W.H. Auden's sulky dismissal of poetry as politically useless – 'poetry makes nothing happen' – can be taken as a measure of his own frustration and disillusionment. It is famously applied to art whenever discussed in the context of politics, but Auden's conclusion says more about Auden than it does about art in general.[10] As a young writer, his career had taken off with a series of poems highly tuned to political fault lines and human suffering. The most politically engaged poet of his generation, he had advocated strongly for intervention in the Spanish Civil War, arguing that this was critical to preventing a wider war against fascism in Europe. Like fellow writers Robert Graves, Stephen Spender, George Orwell, Laurie Lee and Ernest Hemingway, Auden went to Spain to fight. But he didn't stay long. Choosing instead to drive an ambulance, one couldn't be found for him, so he was assigned to write broadcast propaganda. With a transmitter that reached only as far as international volunteers, who were already there anyway, the work was absurd, so he wandered around the Aragon front for a few days before returning to England. Certainly in Spain, Auden had made nothing happen. Instead, he harboured a lifelong ambivalence about groups of all kinds, fearing in both left and right their latent capacity for fascism.

No such ambivalence burdened Picasso. At the beginning of the Spanish Civil War, he had spurned Spanish fascists who hoped to co-opt him and his reputation. When invited by the Republican government to become director of the Prado Museum, he had immediately accepted what was an honorary position. But his chance to make a profound contribution to the Republican cause came in 1937 when asked to paint a large mural for the Spanish Pavilion at the Paris World's Fair.

Early sketches of *Songe et mensonge de Franco* (*The Dream and Lie of Franco*) weren't right. The mural would be enormous – 11 feet high, 20 feet long – and a satirical cartoon strip lampooning the dictator's pretensions was too delicate for so gigantic a canvas. Goya proved an inspiration, but also a high barre: just what kind of impact did he want his painting to make? Time to start painting was running out when, on 26 March 1937, German and Italian fascists bombed the Basque village of Gernika at the behest of Spanish nationalists. In three hours, 1,645 men, women and children were killed and 889 injured. Saturation bombing wasn't new; colonial powers had already deployed it in Africa, Asia and India. But this was the first time that Europeans had experienced for themselves what a war on civilians really meant. Now Picasso knew what to paint.

Over a period of about 10 days, as Parisian newspapers filled with photographs from Spain, Picasso sketched sections of the painting and of its overall structure. With a mind full of images and references, he drew, edited, refined. After two weeks, he started pinning his sketches onto the huge canvas. It didn't quite work. Some areas were too crowded, others too flat. A woman's dress became a collage, with a large patch of coloured wallpaper that was later removed, then finally restored. 'There are forms', Picasso said, 'that impose themselves on a painter. He doesn't choose them. And they stem from an atavism that antedates animal life. It's very mysterious and damned annoying.'[11]

The Spanish Pavilion opened on 12 July 1937. For all that Picasso had a horror of finishing – he associated it with death – he had worked fast. Now hanging in a cool, calm, modern space, the monumental painting was a vast grey and white silent scream. The Republican government that had commissioned it wasn't impressed; when Picasso offered to give them the picture for free, they declined. The German government singled it out as a 'hodgepodge of body parts that any four year old could have painted'.[12] Neither left nor right approved. But a child was overheard saying what many since have thought: 'I don't know what that's meant to be, but it gives me a very queer feeling ... just as if somebody's cut me to pieces.' One of its earliest enthusiasts, Myfanwy Piper, astutely observed, 'The detachment is in the painting, and not in the feeling; that is what gives his abstract pictures life and make *Guernica* a great painting and not just a piece of sentimental propaganda. What happens when the picture is done is, as Picasso points out, quite a different matter.'[13]

What happened next was that the painting went on a fundraising and recruiting tour for Spanish refugees and the International Brigades. Denmark, Sweden, and then London, where it opened at the New Burlington Galleries on the day that the Munich Agreement was signed. Anthony Blunt hated it, deeming it obscure and elitist. But in its potent use of ordinary images, Herbert Read compared it to Goya, Homer, Dante and Cervantes: 'It is only when the commonplace is inspired with the intensest passion that a great work of art, transcending all schools and categories, is born, and being born lives immortally.'[14] The painting received its warmest reception when, on reaching the Whitechapel Gallery in London's East End, it was seen by a broadly working-class audience who paid for their admission with boots fit to be sent to the front.

By the time the picture reached the United States, Madrid had already fallen to the fascists and the Republican army was in retreat, with thousands of refugees fleeing to Europe and

America. Once again, the vast canvas provoked debate: about abstraction, modernism, European influence, art and propaganda. Now that there was no safe home for the work, it had to remain in the USA for the next 40 years.

After the war, the painting became a litmus test for shifting attitudes in Spain. When attitudes softened, Picasso was talked about in his homeland as a national treasure; as they hardened, he was scorned as just another crude communist propagandist. When Picasso's former secretary Jaime Sabartés made a large donation of the artist's work to the city of Barcelona, its gutsy mayor turned a medieval palace into a Picasso Museum, hoping to enliven the city's new cultural centre with a celebration of the region's most famous exile. But just as it was about to open in 1963, the government banned all media coverage. Nevertheless, the museum flourished, and its growing reputation made Franco's government wonder whether they might tempt the picture back, extinguishing its power with their embrace. Picasso steadfastly refused to allow any return until such time as civil liberties were restored in his country.

The Spanish government's skittishness about their world famous painter, who had so powerfully opposed everything they did and stood for, revealed just how fragile their hold on power was. Spanish tourists travelling abroad came home clutching postcards and hanging posters of the great mural while at the same time citizens were jailed simply for receiving a *Guernica* postcard through the post. In 1967, at the beginning of the Prague Spring, the Czech government issued *Guernica* postage stamps, but the Spanish Post Office refused to deliver any letters carrying them. As Franco aged, arguments about the picture revealed how fissiparous Spanish politics were becoming. Picasso's death in 1973 resolved nothing; he had left it to his lawyer to decide when his homeland was fit to receive his great work.

That moment was not reached until 1981, six years after Franco's death. This was also the centenary of Picasso's birth, and diplomatic wrangling to get the picture back was as complex and gnarly as any peace negotiation. When finally, the picture left the Museum of Modern Art, New Yorkers sported black armbands as a sign of farewell. On its arrival in Spain, the huge canvas was welcomed as 'a battle cry against violence, against atrocities, against the horrors of war. ... We see *Guernica* as a pure and simple rejection of brute force.'[15] At the opening ceremony, La Pasionaria (Dolores Ibárruri), the Republican activist and heroine of the Republic, said softly, 'The Civil War is over.' And yet the picture hung behind bulletproof glass.

Today it hangs in Madrid's Reina Sofía museum. Museums around the world have begged to borrow it: in 1980, Nicholas Serota, as the director of the Whitechapel Gallery, tried to use that connection to get the painting back – he felt it was a moment in British history when political artists, or artists who had never considered the political impact of their work, were starting to think about their role within the political firmament of Thatcherism. No deal. Even when the Japanese government asked to borrow it when commemorating the 50th anniversary of the bombing of Hiroshima and Nagasaki they had no luck. It has never left Madrid – although Basque separatists still argue that it should hang in their region or the city of Gernika itself. That it remains so contentious to this day vividly signals how simplistic it is not.

Did *Guernica* make anything happen? In its British tour, it was manifestly part of the roiling debate around Britain's response to fascism, and many argue it stiffened the country's resolve to fight. In the United States, it is widely credited with helping to break down American isolationism. The painting didn't tell people what to think; it helped them to think, to feel solidarity with those already embroiled in war. And in making adults and children feel something for people they would never know, it kept those people human. It still does. Today, versions of the painting can be seen on the streets of Ukraine, in the ruins of Gaza, a potent symbol of the pity of war and our responsibility for it. Just when we are ready to turn away and ignore it, that *Guernica* looks like a broken mirror reminds us simultaneously of our infinite cruelty and our capacity to think.

In the United States, its long sojourn proved a barometer of political rage and frustration. In the 1960s, during the Vietnam War, hundreds of artists petitioned Picasso to take *Guernica* out of the United States, arguing that the country's complicity in bombing civilians meant America had lost the moral stature required to show the work. Others complained that the image had become so famous that it was now meaningless. In an attempt to bring its message back to life, the artist Tony Shafrazi visited the Museum of Modern Art and painted over it: 'Kill Lies All'. Why? He wanted to 'put the painting on the front page of *The New York Times* and of every other newspaper in the world – and that did happen. So it wasn't a hit-and-run, cowardly prank. The critical factor is to realize that the burning, the rage, the inhumanity, and the hatred that is rampant in American culture was really coming to the surface. In a climate like that, nobody pays attention to pretty paintings. The role of art was, I felt, very important and being neglected.'[16]

Another visitor to *Guernica* in the 1960s was Faith Ringgold, who visited the painting frequently with her young daughter. Picasso was a lifelong influence, but of all his work, *Guernica* was her favourite. She struggled to deal with the cognitive dissonance of America, where people were smug, healthy and safe on one street and, just one street over, immersed in violence nobody ever talked about. Surely, she thought, it was the job of artists to make the invisible visible. 'We'd be waiting to go to the movies and suddenly "bam" there's a spontaneous riot. We would never hear anything or see anything about that riot. All over New York, all over America, nothing in the papers about it.'[17] Dissonance like that could (and did) drive people mad.

But not Ringgold. She had a powerful sense of urgency, fighting for racial equality in the 1960s ('there's no reason black power should just be for men') and for women's equality in the 1970s ('there's no reason the women's movement should just be for whites'), and was always driven to make visible what she felt to be ignored. In 1967, mulling over those race riots, she started visiting *Guernica* weekly, and her debt to Picasso stood out loud and clear in her *American People Series #20: Die* (see Figure 18). It shows white and Black New Yorkers fleeing a riot, panic-stricken, two lost children at its centre. Blood is everywhere. Much of its compositional force echoes *Guernica*: the velocity of the horizontal action, the central triangle, the overwhelming sense of chaos, fracture, confusion and fear. At a time when America was in love with abstract art, she chose deliberately to make something emotional and expressive. On seeing it, one woman ran away, terrified.

'I wanted' Ringgold said, 'to finish my American people series with something that was not being talked about and not being dealt with and that was the spontaneous bloody battles that people had in the streets. There's blood on the sidewalk! It's very difficult to paint blood – it feels like you're bleeding. But I had to do it.'[18]

Everywhere she went, she entered galleries to ask if they showed work by Black or female artists. She couldn't find any. How, she wondered, could anyone care about what they didn't see? The blindness had to be wilful, so she determined to change it. When a 1968 retrospective of art from the 1930s at the Whitney Museum of American Art featured no Black artists, she and others protested their absence. In 1970, on discovering how frequently laws protecting the American flag were being abused in order to silence protest, she brought artists together to stage the People's Flag Show, in which every flag made political statements; she got arrested. One of her paintings, *Black Light #10: Flag for the Moon: Die Nigger*, drew attention to the federal funds spent to reach the moon while poor Black American children were going hungry. Commissioned by the National Constitution Center in Philadelphia to produce a work celebrating the 200th anniversary of the Bill of Rights, she wrote the text of the Bill on the red stripes of an American flag. Over the white stripes she put the names of individuals and organizations whom the Act had failed to protect: Martin Luther King. Fannie Lou Hamer. Paul Robeson. Sojourner Truth. It's an eloquent piece about the fragility of freedom.

Speaking in 2018, Ringgold seemed amazed that, after years in which she was invisible, her work now resided in major collections around the world, celebrated for its creative diversity, energy and sheer defiance. 'We are coming into our own', she said. 'We're doing it...' and being seen. In the past decade, work by female, Black, Asian and African artists has been not just shown but also celebrated in a proliferation of exhibits around the world, a revelation to many who, like Ringgold, were more often struck by the absence of their work than any welcome it received. At the age of 90, speaking at a public event at Tate Modern, she was, according to director Frances Morris, the first artist speaking there to get a standing ovation. Her work had catalysed change. It had become a litmus test, too, one that helped to reveal just how much broader, complex and diverse the human capacity to make art has always been. Art is no longer the prerogative only of particular groups or kinds of people. It's no longer possible to believe that the creation of beauty, the capacity to startle, move and challenge us, belongs solely to one place or one people in one time. It comes from everywhere, always, to meet and challenge us all.

How can you care about something you cannot see? Whether drama, imagery or sound, the allure of art (and that includes its ambiguity) draws us in, first curious, then intrigued. That doesn't ensure consensus. But now the ignored thing is out, visible and urgent, it prompts us to imagine, to empathize and to act – together. With so intimate an address, one paradox of art is that it can overcome the private isolation of individual suffering to drive public change.

• • •

Unless they lived through it, few people remember the efforts made to cover up the arrival of AIDS. In the United States, funeral homes frequently refused to serve families of those who had died of AIDS; they just handed out black bin bags instead. The gay community was terrified and marginalized; it was all too easy to dismiss HIV as relevant 'just' to the gay community, nothing anyone else need worry about. Art changed that. Early in 1981, artists like Keith Haring, Robert Mapplethorpe, Derek Jarman and Larry Kramer played a catalytic role in making the new disease visible, demanding action. They had no guarantees of success. Homophobia and public ignorance were rampant, and fear of stigma meant that many AIDS sufferers wanted to keep their disease hidden, which left them even more isolated and desperate.

Governments were prejudiced and apathetic; scientists arrogant, remote and bureaucratic. In the 1980s, the Reagan administration urged people not to worry since the disease was confined, they said, to gay men and intravenous drug users. In the UK, Margaret Thatcher was not told that the victims were largely gay men, because the secretary of state for health, Norman Fowler, feared that the information would give her an excuse to do nothing.

Making the argument for attention, treatment and compassion was, in itself, a claim for equality, demanding that the gay population be accorded the same respect and protection as any other individual. For years that claim was denied.

Even as scientific research began, it became clear that science alone wasn't enough to fight ignorance, fear, prejudice and stigma. In the second year of the epidemic, the playwright Larry Kramer and five colleagues set up Gay Men's Health Crisis (GMHC) to provide trustworthy information about the disease. Then, Kramer told its story. His 1985 play *The Normal Heart* followed the history of GMHC, the patients and cases that its workers encountered on a daily basis; this was a heartbreaking and frightening play, whether you were gay or not. Did we really inhabit a world where people and institutions could be so heartless? What did that say about us?

The scientific establishment had no experience of working with patients – that was the job of drug companies, who were not convinced that there was a lucrative market in AIDS drugs. Patients frequently now knew more than researchers, but institutional and other biases kept the two apart. In 1987, despairing of action, Kramer founded ACT UP (AIDS Coalition To Unleash Power), whose energy focused on massive, public provocations: obstructing the Post Office on tax return day and staging a die-in at St Patrick's Cathedral to protest the church's perverse stance on condoms. These harnessed all of Kramer's stagecraft: carefully selecting audiences and arriving with imagery and events both unexpected and unforgettable. The message became brutally simple: SILENCE = DEATH.

By 1986, Anthony Fauci estimated that there were a million cases in the United States alone. As the mood grew apocalyptic in 1987, the AIDS quilt began – a national invitation for the bereaved to contribute a patchwork panel to commemorate their lost loved ones. Each handmade panel measured 3 × 6 feet, roughly the size of a human grave. Many contained multiple names. In its first year, displayed on the National Mall in Washington DC during the national march for lesbian and gay rights, it was larger than a football field. By 1996 it covered the entirety of the Mall, a vast and visible symbol of a crisis, and a population that many preferred to ignore.

This was also the period when General Idea produced some of their most unforgettable work: the ubiquitous AIDS *Imagevirus* that riffed off Robert Indiana's LOVE logo, and a remarkable installation Magi© Bullet – pill-shaped Mylar balloons filled with helium, all clinging to the ceiling until, one by one, the helium leaked out and a balloon dropped silently to the ground. The art made during the grimmest years of this pandemic took on two emotional modes: loud and furious with frustration, and quiet grief. Conceiving a way through the tragedy had become an urgent, shared act of support, stamina and imagination.

Only in 1996, as a result of constant pressure from ACT UP, together with excruciatingly slow negotiations between the research establishment and the AIDS activists that finally convinced scientists to work directly with patients, did the first effective treatments for AIDS begin to emerge. It took years to get drugs into all the bodies that needed them, and access still isn't as comprehensive as doctors and activists would like. But Kramer's theatrical tactics left a long legacy. After the Parkland high school shooting in February 2018, he taught teenagers how to stage die-ins when they campaigned for gun control. By the end of the year, state legislators had enacted 50 new laws restricting access to guns in the United States.[19] The photographer Nan Goldin, in her campaign against the Sackler family, whose firm she blamed for the oxycontin epidemic, staged beautiful die-ins at museums that had accepted Sackler donations and sponsorships. At the Guggenheim in New York, prescriptions floated down the atrium lined with great works of art: eloquent and terrifyingly sad. In both campaigns, breakthrough research and copious journalism and lobbying had unearthed facts and made them visible: necessary, but not sufficient for action. Was it the artistry, the memorability of these campaigns that tipped the scales? It's impossible to know. What is clear is that action did follow, sometimes in unanticipated ways. The profound achievements of activists, artists and scientists during the AIDS epidemic saved lives, but from 1998 onwards, starting with the Netherlands, there was a cascade of states, countries and territories enacting some form of gay marriage. Where silence had meant death, breaking the silence meant life, with homosexuals now on a more equal footing than ever before in history.

Today the AIDS quilt is the largest ongoing community artwork in the world.[20] At 54 tons, it is now too big and too heavy to be moved or exhibited easily, so it has migrated online, where each panel can be viewed and sections loaned to museums and community spaces. Testifying to the artistry and creativity of each person who contributed to it, this form of gentle collective protest derives its strength and impact from beauty and sheer scale: the visual representative of an entire community. That it is handmade and beautiful is vivid proof that protest need not always be frightening, noisy, harsh; indeed, it is often at its most compelling when it draws in those otherwise uncomfortable with, or excluded from, acts of public demonstration.

Quilting in particular, and textiles in general, have a long history of quiet protest made predominantly by women, using traditionally invisible and underestimated domestic skills to make themselves powerful and visible. Quilting as an art form is found all over the world; for the very poor, it combines personal expressiveness with utility. The now famous Gee's Bend quilters in Alabama produced dazzling works from scraps of shirts, dress hems and worn-out work clothes. The array of colours and the variety of patterns are such that, hung up in front of large windows, they have all the beauty of the finest stained glass. In the variety and freedom of their style, they are vehement: 'I had the power to make this the way I wanted it.'

During the Depression in the United States, Roosevelt's New Deal bought and divided land that had formerly been plantations; the houses built on it were made available to the descendants of slaves. Martha Jane Pettway was what we would now call a community activist, liaising with government officials to make sure her neighbours didn't miss out on New Deal assistance projects. For her, quilting was a source of comfort: 'I don't make them to sell, I just make them and love to sew ... love to quilt.' While her daughter-in-law Loretta Pettway had always looked upon quilting as just another female chore, she changed her mind on moving into a home of her own. 'We only had heat in the living room', she said, 'and when you go out of that room, you need cover ... them quilts done keep you warm.' Her *String-Pieced Quilt* (1960) fashioned a gorgeous piece of abstraction out of men's old clothing (see Figure 19). For many of these women, quilting was simultaneously an expression of community – sewing together – and of individuality – the pattern is all my own. In their making, community and individuality were not opposites.

By 1966, the Freedom Quilting Bee became one of the very few Black-owned businesses in America and it brought economic stability to the area. The visual vigour and variety of these works leaves you in no doubt that they are much more than utilitarian items: they are thoughtful, experimental, playful expressions of independence, the power to create and take seriously whatever one makes, without apology or deference.[21] At the beginning of this century, museums started to notice, collect and exhibit them, but they had been there all along, an affirmation of confidence in their maker's worth.

Since then, the discovery and reinvention of textile art has been explosive. What was previously trivialized as women's work – handicrafts too domestic, too decorative to be art – is now revealed as original, important, inexhaustible in its possibilities. In Poland, in the early 1960s, enormous fibrous works by Magdalena Abakanowicz puzzled and defied Western critics – what were they: paintings? Sculptures? Tapestries? Ironically it was their very *in*utility that finally denoted her work *as* art. Denominated 'abakans', the name encapsulated not just the ferocity and originality of her work, but also acknowledged that the very nature of women's art could redefine what art is and can become. It has been typical of women's art that much progress has occurred outside institutions and centres of power, often in direct conflict with them. Chronic conditions of marginalization, rather than crises, have fuelled collective experiences of change.

'I lived through the 60s, when that was going to be our liberation – but it wasn't', photographer Maggie Murray remembers. 'In the 80s, women were still in the kitchen doing the washing up. We were quite disillusioned, we'd really got the wrong end of the stick as far as everyday life went. And we just started to think it would be better if we worked together, to get some kind of strength in numbers.'

For Murray, the catalytic event was the women's camp at Greenham Common (see Figure 21). In August 1981, 36 women walked from Cardiff to the American airbase in Berkshire to protest against the presence of US cruise missiles in England.

The action involved only women, harnessing their identity as the mothers of future generations to campaign against a catastrophic future for all children. Once again, the invisible was being made visible: in this case, the image of nuclear warheads sitting, primed for use in the midst of the English countryside. Because the site was remote, the reality of the Cold War and the rising possibility of actual war were easy to ignore. What kept the threat in the public mind were women and art.

Murray went back and forth to Greenham, photographing the camp, the women, the art that decorated the encampment, and made the protest visually articulate. 'All the posters and the banners were saying: "imagine what a wonderful world it would be if these things, the missiles, weren't here." As opposed to a message which says, "we hate you, get rid of them." So it showed a real alternative, beautifully.'

What drew nascent filmmaker Beeban Kidron to Greenham was disappointment. She had gone to the National Film and Television School to learn how to change the world, only to find herself surrounded by contemporaries yearning to get rich from advertising. As the only woman in the camera department, she was outnumbered and felt outskilled. With that feeling of 'being rubbish', she agreed to go along with documentary maker Amanda Richardson and hone her hand-held camera skills.

'Well, once we'd been, and once we saw, and once we experienced that immense moment of 30,000 women and the singing around the base and the incredible images they created, I said, "I don't want to go home." And from that moment, we spent more or less continuously seven months at the camp. It was life-changing in terms of having a sense of what was possible, and it made us all much more ambitious in a good way, seeing possibilities we'd never imagined for ourselves and for other people. You were living in a situation where everybody pulled their weight, everybody had a voice, everybody had an ultimate aim that nuclear weapons should not be used in our name in the name of women on British soil.'

'It was an amazing movement', Peter Kennard recalls. A young political artist at the time, he often visited the camp at weekends. 'An amazing visual movement. Those weekends when everyone went down there and covered the whole perimeter with tapestries and banners. This became a great eight-mile montage – and inside you had the concrete bunkers.' The contrasts could not have been more powerful: the weak protesting the forceful. The colourful, ornate, lively banners surrounding brutal, bleak missile silos. Life and death, the imagery of Greenham, framed the human gift of creativity against the human lust for destruction.

Over time, the encampment attracted up to 70,000 women, some staying for years, others coming only at weekends. Men did join but were not allowed to stay overnight – the women believed that kept the camp more peaceful. 'It did feel a very safe place', Murray remembers. 'For lots of women, it felt safer than home. Which is kind of chilling, really. But I never felt there would be any danger except, to be honest, from the police. If you had a camera, you were likely to have it pushed in your face or to be manhandled, literally manhandled. But apart from that it did feel safe because what the women said went. That was what counted. So it was an anti-nuclear protest, an anti-war protest and a feminist protest all at once. And that it stayed so peaceful over so many years, well I think that really said something.'

For a long time mainstream photojournalists ignored the protest, but when they tried to demean it – taking pictures up girls' legs – women seized an opportunity. Murray was one of the founding members of Format, a women-only photographic agency set up to get pictures of women doing more than domestic chores into the mainstream press. Together with Raissa Page, Jenny Matthews and many other female photographers, their work at Greenham revealed an alternative, feminist world: the perimeter fence became an art gallery, decorated with pictures, ribbons, paper cut-outs of people holding hands and everywhere spiderwebs made of yarn woven through the perimeter fence representing the interconnection of life.

'The sort of protests that the women made were very creative. I think I've been to so many demonstrations, which are boring, or they didn't lend themselves to being portrayed visually', says Murray. 'And the most creative thing that I experienced – really one of the great experiences of my life – was on the first of January 1983, when they climbed over the fence, ran across the airfield and danced on the silos. There was no violence; it was cold, it was dark, it was raining on them and it made a beautiful image. There seems to have been a spirit, which was very positive, clearly very imaginative. As if they were saying: imagine what a wonderful world it would be if these things weren't here.' (See Figure 20.)

Above all, Murray remembers the banners. 'The banners were extraordinary, the banners that Thalia Campbell did, were on the fences and on the marches and they really are works of art.' Campbell had been one of the Cardiff marchers. Irked when photographers were more drawn to photographing young women's legs, she decided to distract them with big gorgeous, eye-catching banners (see Figure 22).

'I decided that to get a message across, it had to be beautiful, it had to be well made, and it had to lock into history', Campbell recalled. Her colours had deliberate historic resonance: green and purple for the suffragettes, red poppies reminiscent of sacrifice, the reality of war. 'We were speaking to women in their own language you know? "Girls say no to bombs." "Women's struggle won the vote. Use it for disarmament." "Remembrance is not enough." "Coercion is not government", a quote from Sylvia Pankhurst.'[22] To exiting soldiers, these may have been annoying, but to women arriving at the camp, they were welcome signs. For photographers like Murray, they made dynamic, memorable pictures.

'It was incredible what these women achieved', Murray said. 'When they first started marching, it was all very jokey and dismissive, horrible really. And then it began to get serious and they were taken seriously. And I think that over time it became clear that we weren't just against something – nuclear war – we were *for* something. There was a positive message about a different way to live, peacefully and together.'

For Kidron, having seen the power and effectiveness of women and art, her seven months at Greenham proved life-changing. 'When I got back to film school, after having made *Carry Greenham Home* and it going all over the world and going into cinemas and to the Berlin Film Festival, I decided I wanted to be a director, not a camerawoman. I hadn't known that before. But I felt so much stronger. I have always been a person who started walking towards something before I completely understood it.'

In August 1989, following the Intermediate-Range Nuclear Forces Treaty between the USA and the USSR, the first cruise missiles left Greenham; the last were gone by March 1991. The last protester left the site in September 2000; it is now public parkland. Over its 19 years, the art at Greenham had conveyed many messages: the interconnectedness of human life, which required nuclear disarmament and peace, the positive power of women and children, the overarching need for human beings to work together for the future of those children. Like its sister site, set up at the Seneca Army Depot in upstate New York, Greenham women used art, especially art forms typically denigrated because seen as domestic, to posit an alternative feminist view of protest itself: less rage, more sorrow, less hatred, more love. The full emotional possibilities of art evoke an implicit imaginative optimism: as human beings, we can do, must do, better. Let's try.

'I'd always been an activist, but I started to think that all that activity was a form of defence against feeling', Sarah Corbett explains. She grew up in Liverpool in the 1980s with a deep sense of service, an obligation to leave the world better than she found it. In London, she designed and managed campaigns for big charities; her evenings and weekends were dedicated to political actions. But over the years, she started to have doubts; the aggression implicit in much activism sat uncomfortably with her.

'I was in a meeting one day where we were talking about taking a tank to the big arms conference in London and I'm sitting there wondering: how? Won't it look like an ad? It just made no sense to me. And it got me thinking: why is so much activism so aggressive? Why don't we give people more time to think?'

Going home to Liverpool one weekend – a five-and-a-half hour journey – she realized that she hadn't made anything beautiful for a long time. At the last minute, she picked up a cross stitch kit and when the train movement started to make her feel queasy, she set to work on it.

'And I'd never done cross stitch in my life! But getting the kit out, I realized that I had shaky hands, really tight shallow breaths, this rapid inner monologue going on: can I be an activist? I'm finding this so hard, maybe it's not for me. I saw myself getting so impatient and wound up when threads got tangled! I was so burned out. But now I was doing something comforting while delving into these really difficult questions and doing the repetitive action calmed me down and helped me think through the discomfort. And suddenly, I'm using my hands again and I'm not travel sick.'

'The couple opposite me were watching and they were curious – what you doing? – and I, being an activist geek thought: isn't this interesting, they've initiated a conversation, that doesn't usually happen. If only I were stitching a quote from Gandhi we could have a conversation about peace. ...'

By the time she'd got off the train, Corbett had decided to form the Craftivist Collective – using crafts as a gentle form of protest. Not shaming or shouting at people, but creating environments in which making beautiful objects might help people think together. Like the activist she was, she was driven to make visible what was either invisible or studiously ignored, but she wanted to do so without aggression, expressing her sense of agency and urgency by calmly making beautiful objects.

'At first I called it intimate activism, because that's what it was. Making gifts for people in power, like embroidering hankies that said things like "Don't blow it. Use your power for good".' Working with museums and other art institutions, Corbett found a ready audience of people who had no experience of activism, but who wanted to make an impact without screaming.

One of her first campaigns as a craftivist targeted Marks & Spencer, which, at the time, didn't pay their staff a living wage – not a single high-street retailer did so. But unless you were a shop worker, nobody really noticed that you could have a job and still not be able to feed your family. So Corbett bought 24 handkerchiefs – from M&S – for 24 board members, for each one of whom an individual craftivist designed and stitched images and questions specifically aimed at the board member's life and personal values.

One craftivist, Gemma, made a hanky with the message: 'Kindness is always fashionable and always welcome.' The words were cross-stitched on a patch of fabric from a piece of clothing that her grandmother had bought from M&S decades ago. One of the board members was the trustee of a national garden – he received a hanky stitched with flowers. Another sat on the board of an opera company – his handkerchief had musical notes and a quote from a musician. This was the beginning of a long, careful and graceful campaign, that aimed to meet company decision makers where they were and speak to the best in them. It initiated a series of longer, more intimate conversations that ended, a year later, with M&S announcing that they would pay their workers above the living wage.[23]

Since then, Corbett has supported and encouraged groups around the world in developing the fine art of gentle protest. In 2022 one hundred flocks of bright yellow cloth canaries stood out at COP 26, a quiet and beautiful warning of the natural world threatened by climate change. The point, she says, was not just a great picture but a deep experience: the thousands of hours of conversations between craftivists making their canaries together, not feeling alone but exploring how to change lifestyles and how else to disseminate their sense of the urgency of now. The art, she believes, makes a difference, but just as important, perhaps more important, is the impact of making it on the artist. Making art changes you. Making it together changes many of you.

'What I love about art', Corbett says, 'is that it is a catalyst for an emotional response. I don't want it to tell me what to think but when you're making something beautiful, it helps you think. And when you're with other people who've come together to make something beautiful because of concerns they all care about, you have different conversations. There is always an action to take, asking powerholders to shift, changing people's minds, policy, law. …'

Corbett is routinely asked to prove that craftivism works. Familiar with the gamut of theories of change, she says it is arrogant for any activist to say that doing X achieves Y. Of course she's thrilled when a major business changes its policy, but she is just as committed to the idea that craftivism plants new ideas in people's heads. Many of her projects and events 'are seeds, like resources to educate and empower people to use our gentle protest tools to create their own change, in their local context.' For her, making something beautiful is a meaningful way to remind people of the agency they have always had. In this her approach speaks to new research showing that it isn't changing beliefs that drives people to action, but the reverse: doing something different changes beliefs.[24]

'The act of making something that nobody asked for is a statement in itself', is how Peter Kennard puts it. Britain's foremost political artist, he has been making political art for over 50 years.

Propaganda, he says, tells people what to do whereas political art breaks through the surface of things. In his photomontages, this is often literally true. On the floor of his studio lie old broadsheet newspapers; on top of them, Kennard has superimposed the faces of refugees. As the photographic images fight through the newsprint, the deliberate obscurity of their combination slows down my response; I have to look closely to understand what I'm seeing. The face looks back at me, making me think about all those people flying through the news cycle whom we never stop to think of as people like us. But not here. I can't help but stop, to think about this woman, how little I know or think about her (see Figure 23), how little I consider her life going on at the same time as mine.

Kennard trained as a painter but he has become a master of photomontage, juxtaposing a familiar image with an unexpected one to create a third meaning. A tagline for *The Times* newspaper in the 1980s ('Have you ever wished you were better informed?') accompanied the picture of a skeleton reading *Protect and Survive*, the government's booklet informing citizens what to do in case of a nuclear war. After his time visiting Greenham, considering classic images of the English countryside, Kennard took Constable's painting, *The Hay Wain*, and replaced the hay in the painting with missiles. The visual gag took off and was soon turned into posters and postcards. From time to time, he would take postcards of his work to the National Gallery (where the original *Hay Wain* hangs) and interleave them with Constable postcards; the idea of tourists taking home his montage by accident tickled him. The biggest challenge for political artists, he said, is always to get the work seen outside art galleries, so that it catches people unawares. Although his work sits inside the British Museum, the V&A and the Tate, Kennard never made much money from it. Most was designed for billboards or posters: to be out in the world catching people's eyes.

At the Imperial War Museum his *Decoration* paintings combine digital prints of American and British military honours with oil and pigment (see Figure 24). What remains are images of frayed and mangled ribbons and, where the medals should be, wounded faces, bagged heads and sometimes nothing at all. If you look at them for a time, you can't but imagine who these missing faces belonged to, but in being reminded of them, you may also see your own, our own, indifference. This protest is far from simplistic; the images urge us to think not just about the war and the real people drawn into it, but of the hardness of heart, the residue that war leaves behind in us.

'I talked to lots of ex-servicemen and they were really into this project', Kennard remembered. 'You see, they never thought they did what they did for medals, or for rewards.' This understated, quietly devastating anti-war work is not anti-soldier; it is a dignified memorial mourning their sacrifice. It can't but make you think of their fear and their suffering. No wonder Kennard cites Goya as an influence.

'If it's art', Kennard say, 'it is because it is done freely. It isn't being dictated, but encourages people to think, to be part of doing something. All forms of art show that there is still a human spirit that hasn't been bashed down by capital and mass media.'

Much of his work is now preserved in the books *@earth* and *Visual Dissent*. Their chronology tracks an age of asymmetry: children in casinos amidst piles of poker chips, a half-remembered image of Andrew Wyeth's *Christina's World* where fields have been replaced with collapsed oil refineries. These are bleak realities to live with; was Kennard never tempted towards cynicism?

'I think making is inherent in all of us. So it's a good thing to do', he says. 'I work with pensioners. They say "I've never done anything like this since I was at school" but as soon as they start, things happen. You surprise yourself.' Then a long, thoughtful pause. 'If I didn't do this work, I'd feel I was going along with the status quo. If I am making something, then I feel I am doing something. One of the things I *can* do is respond to the world; that's why I started doing it originally, because just responding to my own life didn't seem enough. I feel I am doing something in relation to the suffering of the world. Bearing witness.'

• • •

> No not under a foreign sky,
> Not under the shelter of alien wings –
> I was with my people then,
> there where my people were doomed to die.[25]

The words are from Anna Akhmatova's 'Requiem'. She wrote it between 1935 and 1961, a period during which her publications were suppressed by the Soviet government. Before Stalin's Great Purge, she had been one of the country's most cherished poets, but by the time she wrote 'Requiem', she only just survived by doing occasional translation work and depending on the generosity of friends, family and fans. Her first husband, Nikolai Gumilev, was executed by the Soviet police, her common-law husband Nikolay Punin died in the Gulag and her son Lev spent 20 years in and out of prison camps because he was her son. Akhmatova's was the experience of millions, and although many poets fled, she stayed, steadfastly refusing to abandon her country, her people and her language. As an artist, she felt it was her job to bear witness, that the usefulness of her art was to keep clearly in focus what was denied or erased all around her. 'The worship of her memory in the Soviet Union today, undeclared but widespread, has, so far as I know, no parallel', Isaiah Berlin wrote. 'Her unyielding passive resistance to what she regarded as unworthy of her country and herself transformed her into a figure, not merely in Russian literature, but in the Russian history of our time.'[26]

Under constant surveillance, her flat bugged for years, Akhmatova worked secretly on 'Requiem', a poem that bears witness to mothers standing outside the Leningrad prison waiting for news of their sons. The poem was dangerous – friends memorized it, making sure afterwards to burn the scraps of paper on which she'd shared it with them – but she had to write it. That sense of compulsion is common to much political art, the vehement refusal to normalize terror. Even when traces of burned paper might lead to death, Akhmatova and her friends staunchly preserved the truth only art can tell.

Instead of a Foreword

During the terrible years of the Yezhov Terror, I spent seventeen months in the prison queues in Leningrad. One day somebody in the crowd 'identified' me. Then a woman with lips blue from the cold who was standing behind me, and of course had never heard of my name, came out of the numbness which affected

us all and whispered in my ear – (we all spoke in whispers there):
'Can you describe this?'
I said: 'I can!'
Then something resembling a smile slipped over what had once been her face.[27]

In her raw account of the purges, Akhmatova stands, like the Virgin Mary beside the body of Christ, grieving with mothers in front of a Leningrad prison, weeping and afraid for their lost sons and husbands. An unpredictable mixture of stanzas and verses, the words barely hang together, as overcome with horror as she is herself. Torn between love and pain, hope and despair, the words seem to gasp for breath from line to line. In the smile that Akhmatova exchanges with the woman in front of the prison is a flicker of spirit, a promise that she will not break. Unyielding in what she insists on seeing and recording, Akhmatova witnesses the scene in the legal sense – her pain and grief vouch for the truth of it. In reading her words, we become witnesses too. The act of remembrance is an act of resistance.

> VII. Sentence
> The stone word fell
> on my still beating breast.
> Never mind, I was prepared,
> somehow I'll come to terms with it.[28]

In 1958, the Soviet government began to relent, allowing her to write and to publish again. But when her *Collected Works* appeared that year, it did not include 'Requiem'; she sensed it was still too dangerous. Only in 1987, two years before she died, was it finally made available to the Russian people.

The problem that art poses for the purveyors of certainty is that it won't submit. It demands a dialogue, unsettling cozy assumptions: about ourselves, our lives, each other, about what to believe and what to feel. It demands that we think for ourselves. For those seeking to force-fit human life into predictable behaviours, feelings and convictions, this is an anathema. That, historically, writers in Russia were worshipped as truthtellers, made (and makes) their artists even more dangerous, but it would be a mistake to impute this view to Russians alone; the propensity of authoritarian governments to attack and terrorize artists, to scorn, repudiate or suppress their work implicitly acknowledges the power of art to make things happen.

If one of the functions of political art is to provoke alternative explorations of the present, another is to stimulate imaginative challenge to our understanding of the past, taking a stand against the desire, even the biological impulse, to forget responsibility, pain and guilt. Art remains, not just as information (although it is a form of information), but by proliferating questions about the past, a crucial bulwark against sentimentality and jingoism.

This is what Steve McQueen's film *Grenfell* gives us. In 24 minutes, we see and hear London, its birdsong, pollution and traffic. On one level, the film is as simple as can be: just a camera circling and circling the burnt-out tower where 72 people died in the fire. No words. No music. We just look. With nothing to guide us, we turn inward, imagining who lived there, whether they escaped, their terror, ambivalence – stay or run? – the loneliness – who to ask? Nothing happening is something happening. Plastic covering the building billows in waves against the scaffolding. We can't see inside but we don't want to intrude; there are ghosts enough in our heads. The continuing silence forces us to think, to feel and to pay tribute to people we wish we could have saved.

Much of McQueen's work is in the same vein. His artwork *Queen and Country*, commissioned by the Imperial War Museum, was a cabinet like a catafalque, holding prototype sheets of stamps, each featuring portraits of British casualties of the Iraq War – stamps the Post Office refused to issue. At a time when many in the UK wanted to forget all about Northern Ireland, his film *Hunger* remembered the IRA hunger strikers who had died in prison. *Twelve Years a Slave* shifted an overlooked slave memoir from the archives to mainstream cinema. In *Small Axe*, McQueen brought into British homes stories about West Indian life in London that most Londoners had forgotten or never known. The consoling narrative portraying the Dutch as passive resisters to the German Occupation was wholly upturned by *Occupied City* – over four hours, McQueen's film showed how the Netherlands lost 75 per cent of Dutch Jews to concentration camps, the highest percentage of any country occupied by Nazi Germany. These works don't pussyfoot around; they're not out to please or to sell, cajole or comfort. But neither do they take sadistic delight in the horrors they show. Without art, McQueen has said, we are powerless. No longer seduced by nursery histories, uncertainty is the motivating force for addressing new questions, considering freshly informed responses, thinking anew.

The smile that Akhmatova glimpsed on a stranger's face said: if you can write this, that means it did happen and therefore can be remembered. Here art is the last hope of the powerless. That is why language matters: it is, as the critic George Steiner wrote, 'the main instrument of man's refusal to accept the world as it is.'[29] He was writing about words, but he could have been thinking about any language: musical or visual. To defy the world by remembering what is excruciating to see and tempting to ignore demands fierce imaginative courage.

The intent is not comfort, the packing up and tidying away of atrocity or the aestheticization of horror. 'Requiem' challenges us not to be heartless; worse than the disasters from which these voices spring would be to feel nothing. The poem lives in the liminal space between witnesses' feelings of responsibility – neither Akhmatova nor the strange woman with blue lips can say they didn't know – and their own helplessness. Warning or atonement, the only way to maintain a human conscience is fully to face what occurred and to stand with the weak. Which is exactly what Shostakovich did in his 'Symphony No 13'.

'I feel now that I am a Jew. .../I feel that I am Dreyfus. .../I feel that I am Anne Frank ...' proclaim the opening verses of the first of five poems by Yevtushenko that Shostakovich set in what came to be known as the 'Babi Yar Symphony'. Neither composer nor poet was Jewish; their solidarity derived from a shared experience of terror. Both men knew what Shostakovich described as the 'desperate fear of *not being fearless*'.

Better than anyone, Shostakovich felt how often he had failed to be fearless; both decorated and denounced, he had made so many concessions to the Soviet state, bent, strained and contorted himself and his music for both to survive. On applying for membership of the Communist party, he wept. This man who had lost friends, family and colleagues in the Great Terror, who had kept a bag packed, ready for the moment he would be sent to the camps, had survived, but at the cost of his conscience.

What drove him, in 1960, to make a stand against Stalinist Terror and anti-semitism? Some kind of crisis. Perhaps the greater bravery he discerned in Yevtushenko, who was a generation younger and whose poems dared to confront the Soviet government's steadfast refusal to memorialize the massacre of Kyiv Jews, communists and Romani. Perhaps a sense that the political mood was changing. Perhaps, too, a desire for atonement, when he asked Yevtushenko for an additional poem that denounced the failure to speak out, remaining silent 'when we should have screamed'. That he wrote a symphony so ferocious in its condemnation of his country's conformity, careerism and anti-semitism was obviously, deliberately subversive. 'I am not expecting this work to be understood', he wrote, 'but I cannot *not* write it.'[30]

Nobody knew better the risks he took. Stalin might be dead, a thaw might have begun, but the night before its premiere, Khrushchev, denying the existence of anti-semitism in the Soviet Union, demanded to know why Yevtushenko felt compelled to write about Babi Yar. Tensions ran high. One singer dropped out. Hours before the concert was due to start, Shostakovich was summoned to a private meeting with the Central Committee. Before going in, he broke down in tears. But when asked to cancel the concert, this time the man who had been afraid of his own fear refused.

TV crews hoping to broadcast the concert were sent away. The published programme no longer contained the texts of Yevtushenko's poems. Shostakovich feared audience catcalls – but his work was met with cheers and a standing ovation.

Not for the first time, an artist had managed to articulate the conscience of the country. Everyone in the Soviet Union had made compromises; the least they could do now was to acknowledge their weakness and its cost. But after a further three performances in Minsk, the symphony was unofficially banned.

It still touches nerves. In May 2023, at a Boston performance, the Russian bass singer, Ildar Abdrazakov withdrew at the last moment; Ukraine was very much in mind.[31] And according to the critic and historian Jeremy Eichler, 'Babi Yar' has never once been performed in Austria.[32]

Shostakovich said he wanted to remind his audience of conscience, to alert us to our own conformity. The power of music is such that it can draw us in to consider what we don't want to see. A protest against amnesia, it offers a gift: the chance to retrieve our humanity. This is what Shostakovich's audience cheered: having been given a way to feel, together, and to relocate that place where morality should live.

It's a strange feature of political art that it can fuse anger, hatred and shame with beauty. Nowhere is that more incandescent than in the song 'Strange Fruit', written by the white Jewish American poet Abel Meeropol. 'I wrote "Strange Fruit" because I hate lynching, and I hate injustice, and I hate the people who perpetuate it', he said.

The song has a slow, mysterious allure. Its tune gorgeous and its subject grotesque, the contradiction draws you in and keeps you listening. At first, the words are so oblique: a factual account that never names the picture it paints. You have to listen so carefully to understand what its subject is. That we, as listeners, must provide the hideous word enlists us co-conspirators in the suppressed rage of the melody. The tautness of its rhythmic dignity and defiant ambiguity puts the singer in total command of the audience. No wonder Billie Holiday claimed to have written it; she lived it as she sang it and she made it unforgettable. Simultaneously you want to hear it again and you never want to hear it again. Lacking a single word of protest, it has been called by many the greatest protest song ever written. And all it says is: look.

Holiday's performance is so magisterial that few dared take it on in her lifetime. Others have attempted it – Tori Amos, John Martyn, Dee Dee Bridgewater, Sting – but only Nina Simone has ever come close to owning it. Holiday's performance is deeply internalized; probing her own wounds, she scarcely acknowledges an audience but seems puzzled by a lifetime of pain. Nina Simone is different; she sings right at us with a tough, fearless, rage.

She was an activist through and through. 'I choose to reflect the times and the situations in which I find myself. That to me is my duty. I don't think you have a choice. How can you be an artist and *not* reflect the times?'[33] She hadn't always felt this way. A childhood prodigy, she had hoped to become America's first Black classical pianist. But that dream collapsed with her most personal experience of racism, when she was rejected by the Curtis Institute of Music. Instead, she had to support herself playing show tunes in crummy cocktail bars, changing her name from Eunice Waymon to Nina Simone so her preacher mother wouldn't know where she hung out. That highly successful career brought money and fame, but also a lingering sense of shame and unease; what was this all for? She had never wanted to be just an entertainer and she was afraid of not being fearless.

The bombing of the 16th Street Baptist Church in Alabama and the assassination of civil rights leader Medgar Evers in Mississippi changed all that. Now she lost her fear, writing the song 'Mississippi Goddam' in under an hour; in its energy and driving beat, you feel her urgency. The song doesn't mess around – there is no innuendo. She was sick of conforming, being told that if she was good, patient and ladylike, eventually ... well, eventually she might be tolerated. She called her tune a show tune for a show that hadn't been written yet, and she was fed up with being lied to. The song came from a 'rush of fury, hatred and determination' and she called it 'Mississippi Goddam' because that's what she meant, and what everyone around her felt. 'We all wanted to say it', Dick Gregory later said, 'She said it.'[34] Many consider it the first song of the civil rights movement.

Cursing was not allowed on radio stations at the time, so the records were returned, many broken in two. But Simone sang it at all her concerts, including when she played Carnegie Hall. She had built a following and now she knew how to use it. Throughout her career she sang and wrote political songs: 'Backlash Blues', 'Four Women', 'Revolution' and 'To Be Young, Gifted and Black' are all her compositions. But it feels as though 'Strange Fruit' was meant for her; you can hear her simmering grief from the opening line to the tremulous last note. This is no internalized memory; she is handing the shame of lynching over to us to figure out. It took a long time; by the time she died in 2003, lynching was still not illegal in the United States. That would have to wait until 2022.

Simone's vulnerable, belligerent, beautiful impatience inspired and validated Black people, women, anyone at the sharp end of false promises, exclusion, injustice, prejudice and violence. The power of her voice and of her songs threw down a challenge: you don't have to live with her, she insisted in 'Mississippi Goddam'; she just wanted equality. So when, the song asks, will that happen? Don't tell me to be patient; patience will only bring more tragedy. Can't you see the mess we're in?

Making art out of disaster is a defiant statement in itself, a refusal to be silenced or to be afraid. The drive artists have to make something of these emotions is not just force of habit but also an impulse to reconcile cognitive dissonance, to bridge the gap between reality and the consolatory fictions that justify the status quo. That this compulsion, often at great personal risk, is experienced as duty reveals how deeply artists assume responsibility for everything they see. All the curiosity, the meandering and the night walks demand a response. Implicit in that runs the most basic optimism: a fundamental belief that, however uncertain the future, it can be made better only by looking at the world with clear, unflinching eyes.

Not everybody wants to see so clearly. As Simone insisted on injecting politics into her performing career, she steadily lost audiences, income and confidence. Like many activists, she burned out. But her legacy did not.

Half a century after 'Mississippi Goddam', Josette Bushell-Mingo wrestled with all the same issues that Simone had confronted – how to accelerate change, how to contain the vast emotions of anger and grief that inequality provokes – and, like Simone, she wasn't prepared to shut up and conform. Bushell-Mingo is a highly accomplished Olivier award-winning actor, theatre founder and director. In 2001, she launched the PuSh International Performing Arts Festival that strove to put Black creators at the centre, rather than the margins, of major British theatre and arts institutions. For this, in 2006, she was awarded an OBE. For 13 years she ran Sweden's National Touring Deaf Theatre and became the first woman to hold the position of head of acting at Stockholm University of the Arts. Returning to the UK she is now the principal of the Royal Central School of Speech and Drama in London.

Even as a young artist, she was known for doing work that other Black actors wouldn't do: political theatre, physical theatre, devised work. For as long as she can remember, she has been negotiating, reconsidering questions of racism, identity and resistance. These became more urgent and inescapable during the 'summer of death' in 2015 when #BlackLivesMatter emerged in response to the police killing of Black American men. Bushell-Mingo now had power, influence – but how should she use it? What impact could she make, and how?

'I didn't ask to do the story of me and Nina Simone', Bushell-Mingo says. 'I had to do it. I don't play Nina. But sometimes she comes in, and as an extraordinary activist female icon composer, she asked herself the same question, which I detect, which we all must ask at some point, living in the political times we are: Who are we going to be and what do we stand for? And what are we prepared to give up?'[35]

'The hardest thing as artists is to believe that things in our lifetime won't change. I kept thinking of that picture of Martin Luther King with his head in his hands and saying to myself: get up, keep going. We still believe we are isolated, but we aren't. We never were. We never are. That's why witness is so important. To say I was there. I saw that. It's a huge responsibility. I didn't know what to do with this feeling, this responsibility. But I kept thinking of Nina. Some kind of mirror?'

'Nina once said of her relationship with fellow black Americans, "my job is to make them curious enough, or persuade them by hook or crook, to get more aware of themselves and where they came from, what they are into, and what is already there – and just to bring it out." This is what compels me to compel them and I will do it by whatever means necessary.'

More than 30 years later, what did that mean for Bushell-Mingo? She set to work devising a one-woman show that, at first, appears to be a conventional concert of Simone's much-loved songs. She comes onstage as Nina the entertainer, big hair, big earrings. She sings 'Revolution' wonderfully. But then she breaks off, interrupting herself to talk to the Nina in her mind.

'I'm sorry, Nina. I can't do this anymore. I can't sing that song anymore. Revolution. The definition of revolution is to revolve. Which means you end up right back in the same place. As if the revolution was a car stuck in the mud. The wheels keep turning and we keep going nowhere.'

What keeps springing back into her mind is 17-year-old Laquan McDonald, shot dead with 16 bullets in 13.5 seconds by a Chicago policeman in 2014. She stamps angrily on the stage floor, 16 times. Finally, she locates the question she's been searching for: 'How the fuck did we come to a time when we had to *say* that black lives matter?'

On stage, Bushell-Mingo is a formidable presence; statuesque, energetic and powerful, you can tell she used to be an athlete. With the facility to shift in an instant from charm to challenge, she can be (as Nina was) both captivating and intimidating. But having stopped singing, where will she go next? The audience is uncomfortable, unsure how much of what they see is planned, intentional, and how much might be impromptu and out of control. Who is talking here: Nina Simone or Josette Bushell-Mingo? They inhabit, for now, the same body.

'I've been contemplating' she tells her audience, 'the act of forgiveness. Or to move on and exist in a society which continuously ridicules, spits upon, mocks, threatens, assaults, beats and disrespects or downgrades us. Revenge. And forgiveness. For me being a Black artist, is to exist somewhere between those words as if forgiveness would be a room or a moment or a purpose. Forgiveness is fluid and constantly changing, depending on whether you are the perpetrator or the victim. How can I forgive when there's no justice?'

A clip of Simone singing from 'Strange Fruit'. And then a film clip of Simone: 'If I had my way, I'd have been a killer. I would have had guns and given them violence for violence and shotgun for shotgun. If I'd had my way. Because I was never a non-violent person.'

'Is that what's needed now?' Bushell-Mingo asks herself. Asks the audience. Onstage, she toys with ideas of revenge, telling Black members of her audience that they can leave but the white people must remain. Let's imagine, she says to them, that she has a gun. Right here. Right now. Audience members become very uneasy. Does she mean this? Is it part of the act? If she had a gun, what would happen next, she asks. The police would come. Her husband would come ('he's white by the way', she tells them). Then her two kids. They would all ask her not to shoot anyone. She loves them.

The show takes the audience down a labyrinth of unexpected turns and possibilities; they feel the trap of rage and grief that she is caught in. A trap that they are in, too. The show is constructed to separate: audience members of African descent will always feel safe and white audience members will realize that the show is not going to be a jazzy tribute gig with a few drinks and cool tunes, but a journey that they didn't expect, having to confront the politics, the world, the violence from which Nina Simone's music sprang. What the songs meant to her. What they still mean today. The audience have to hear the songs afresh, to understand why they aren't just show tunes and why singing them is so difficult for Bushell-Mingo. Because she can't perform them without the entire panoply of the civil rights movement, the Black Lives Matter movement, raging around in her head. The audience sits, uncomfortable, as she is. Unsure what she will decide.

When she's ready, Bushell-Mingo walks offstage, puts on her Afro wig and gold shoes and comes back to sing. Not knowing what to expect, the mood – alarm, uncertainty, anxiety, confusion – hasn't changed.

'My mother used to say', she told me, '"Stay in the valley. Don't try to crawl up the sides." I don't run away from it. From that place, in the valley, I sing these songs which I hope the audience will now listen to differently. I sing them to stay there. In that moment.'

So many of Simone's songs have been used for car ads, for perfume commercials. But that isn't how we hear them now. Bushell-Mingo sings them where they come from, each one rising to a crescendo. The last song, once used at the Superbowl to sell Ford cars, is Simone's 'I Wish I Knew How It Would Feel To Be Free'.

At the end of most performances, a standing ovation. Then a post-show discussion. A young Black woman in Manchester says it's the first time she's been to the theatre; she asks how comfortable it is to present such a realistic image of Black culture in front of a multicultural audience? Bushell-Mingo is fine with it. 'It is the complexity of our existence, the complexity of adjusting and moving in white spaces. That's okay but it has to be acknowledged, accepted that it is a negotiation.' Another simply thanks her: 'The important message tonight is that you can be pro-Black, but that doesn't mean you're anti-white. We are just proud of who we are and we shouldn't be afraid to say that. So thank you.'

The show is cathartic. Why? Because truths have been spoken. Not just reported – none of the facts are new – but felt, integrated into our experience. Because the audience was able to see and understand the frustration of being stuck in that loop of impossible questions: to remember and forgive? To forget and forgive? Impossible to take action. Impossible not to take action. What action? Being paid the compliment of candour. We would all love to know how it would feel to be free.

Bushell-Mingo's exploration of herself and Nina Simone is very delicately calibrated, daring, mindful, full of anger but not abusive, alert to the experiences and perspectives it tangles with. But sometimes such calibration is not always the case with political art. Sometimes it just happens.

In 2014, the producer and songwriter Pharrell Williams was working on Kendrick Lamar's third album. He knew he'd just written a great beat and a hook for the rapper, but nothing much seemed to come of it. Williams was impatient to hear what it would become.

'The beat sounds fun', Lamar recalled, 'but it's something else inside those chords that Pharrell put down ... it feels like it could be more of a statement than a certain tune'. 'Pharrell and Sam Taylor put pressure on me: "when you going to do it, when you going to do it?" Pharrell knew the record was special. Sam knew the record was special. They probably knew it before I even had a clue.'

Taking time to hear what the music wanted from him, Lamar couldn't find the words. For six months he mulled it over. He spent a lot of time, he says, 'talking to kids': 'It put the pressure on me to challenge myself and to think and focus. ... Eventually I found the right words, There was a lot going on – and still to this day – and I wanted to approach it: uplifting but aggressive, not playing the victim but still having that "we're strong."'[36]

What Lamar found, eventually, became the song 'Alright'. The facts of the lyrics are dark – hard times, painkillers, murderous police, rage, evil, self-destruction – but the chorus – Alright! – is triumphant. Defiant. Even joyful. Released in 2015, almost instantly taken up by protest marchers, by 2020 it had become the *de facto* anthem of the Black Lives Matter movement. What made the song a great song wasn't just Williams' beat and hook, not just Lamar's words, and certainly not strategic planning. The crowd and the times made the song, discovered and adopted its insistent, euphoric, defiant optimism just at the moment they needed it.

• • •

There are many who argue that all art is a form of protest. I'm not sure I agree, but I never much care for semantic arguments about categories. What I am more confident of is that, without the capacity to derive from a myriad of anomalies and ambiguities alternative pictures of what life could hold, without the stamina, patience, humility and courage to explore and invent, we leave ourselves at the mercy of those who choose, or seek to enforce, certainty at any cost. Through the ages, what political art and artists see in uncertainty is a moment when we can (or must) think for ourselves, not a nuisance or a burden but an opportunity not to be missed.

Wandering, taking time to pay attention to the undervalued or overlooked, means you will see what others don't. Patterns emerge and gradually, with them, intent and energy. Agency, the demand to take action, grows until there is nothing to do but begin. This is a dominant characteristic of making art. It is also always the dominant characteristic of those who seek a fairer, freer, safer world. Uncertainty is never vanquished; rather, it is overwhelmed by the gravitational pull of glimpsed alternatives. Who among us would not like to know how it feels to be free?

RAFTS

Safe, only safe I feel
When free, free to truly be
When rain falls slow
Around. ...

I can't tell who is singing. A teenager's bedroom. She exits
an American house to go on a wandering walk. Cut to Rory
Pilgrim playing the harp, intent, with an eight-part chamber
orchestra. A choir sings and we see a man, never named,
who describes a tree whose insides have been ripped out.
Yet it lives on. The man fits himself inside its blasted trunk and
can feel protected. Which is weak and which is strong? For
just over an hour, this collage of music, voices, meditations on
fragility and strength unfolds without handrails or signposts.
No narrative but it is a story. No obvious structure but ripples
of meaning. Once we drop our information-seeking instincts,
we are free to be anyone, everyone, in this piece.

RAFTS is a film, an oratorio of seven songs, an exhibition
of drawings made by the film's participants and by Pilgrim.
They have always been interested in languages; learning
Estonian not through necessity but as an form of enquiry:
who might I be in this tongue? And in RAFTS they use every
language they have – painting, dance, poetry, animation,
nature, song, text, live performance, prayer – woven together
like tapestry, entwining vulnerability with strength. A raft is a
fragile form of transport in times of escape. We all need them:
fragile vessels that we are, they take us from place to place,
moment to moment. Anything can be a raft: a garden, an
exquisitely precise painting, a dance. We find rafts in trees, in
song, in being together and being alone. We can be rafts for
each other.

Each song is a seed from which ideas and thoughts
proliferate: stories of darkness and light, being lost and being

found. We are borne along by the music and by people who open themselves to us. In showing us their vulnerability, they reveal their strength. Imagination, Pilgrim says, is a support structure; it lets us dream aloud.

Exhibited alongside three other artists shortlisted for the Turner Prize in 2023, the film showed in a darkened room. By the end, many are in tears, not sad but moved. How did we get so close to people we have never met? The film has been a raft for its viewers, a source of solace, taking us to places we too often ignore, in ourselves and in others. Care is a form of activism, coming from a place of joy, embracing nature.

And if you bring me your flowers
I'll keep them safe for you
So just bring me your flowers
I'll keep them safe like you.

Epilogue:
the benefits of uncertainty

A final thought experiment.

Realizing in the 1970s the reality of climate change, scientists reach out to artists. They know they have a dire warning to make, so terrifying that they can anticipate denial, rejection, campaigns to prove them wrong. Data alone won't inspire the scale and scope of the change that is needed.

In talking to artists, they come to see that the crisis isn't just about numbers and chemistry; it must also be about hope, home and renewal. It's about being afraid – but taking action anyway. Neither the scientists nor the artists are daunted by uncertainty, but they acknowledge that many people are. And so together they forge stories and images that change people's relationship with nature from one of dominance and aggression to one of respect, love and collaboration. Creativity flourishes: new ways to think about how we live, new means of achieving them together. They find joy in the work, in each other and in nature. And balance is restored.

• • •

Like most thought experiments, it's a simple fantasy. But it reveals how far we've come from where we need to be. From a disintegrating world to an integrated one. From division, calculation and despair to one of inspired individual and collective invention. It isn't just that we need mindsets and habits capable of staring into uncertainty with all the pragmatism and optimism that artists put into action daily. We cannot live without them.

As every parent, teacher and PISA researcher knows, everyone can be creative. That's how we start in life but too much gets lost along the way. We need to retrieve and retain the curiosity, energy and initiative we are born with. Schools start out doing this but need to keep going, as artists do: integrating the arts into everything they do, stepping off the treadmill, dropping the security blanket of goals, targets and incentives to include in their ambition the proliferation of creativity as a dynamic, resilient approach to life. Institutions and companies will find their workforce less frightened and frustrated if they can see their colleagues as a source of ideas and invention rather than wayward children to be surveilled and bribed into obedience. There is no simple recipe, no single path to the new ways of living and working that could sustain us; we want a proliferation of these now.

Individually, we need to take this to heart, rejecting the salesmanship, propaganda and technologies purporting to save us the trouble of experiencing life for ourselves. Seize the freedoms we have and use them to wander, notice, listen, enjoy developing our own thoughts, exploring new paths, alone and together. Surrender to our native curiosity to try new people, places and ideas and to practise the conversations that now frighten us. The rewards are great: recuperation, resilience, energy, delight and growth. Yes, we need institutional change, but fundamentally we need a mindset shift: less intimidated by uncertainty, recognizing in it our chances for freedom, imagination, connection and possibility.

Talking to Michael Spence at UCL, he reminded me that his institution had been founded in order to admit to a university people who could *not* sign the 39 Articles, the defining statements of doctrines and practices of the Church of England. England's oldest universities had required this since the English Reformation, believing that to live well in a community required that everyone affirm the same beliefs. In 1826, UCL was founded based on a new idea: that you need divergent ideas to live well together, that to avoid the disenfranchisement of conformity required the curation of pluralism, the capacity for people to think differently while working together. 'If liberal democracy is going to work', Spence said, 'our students need those skills. And a humanities education will give it to you.' Such pluralism is as essential now in our public and private lives as it is in the natural world.

Neither fear of uncertainty nor fantasies of perfect control should make us abandon the creative agency we are born with. The great multitude of ideas and styles, subjects and themes, with which artists enrich the world, is, and has always been, as fundamental to human flourishing as diversity is to nature. There is no predetermined script. The reinvigoration of human creativity isn't a small task, but we begin with the necessary ingredients. We just have to use them. And keep going.

Endnotes

Prologue

1   Nakortoff, K. (2023) '"Imagine Westminster under water": Stricter tests needed to see how City copes with climate disasters', *The Observer*, 24 September. Available from: www.theguardian.com/business/2023/sep/24/stricter-tests-city-copes-climate-disasters [Accessed on 7 October 2024].

2   Grupe, Dan W. and Nitschke, Jack B. (2013) 'Uncertainty and anticipation in anxiety: An integrated neurobiological and psychological perspective', *Nature Reviews Neuroscience*, 14: 488–501, doi: 10.1038/nrn3524.

3   Although this has attracted a great deal of attention recently, it's far from a new discovery. The first academic paper demonstrated this phenomena in the 1970s; see Ball, Thomas S. and Vogler, Roger E. (1971) 'Uncertain pain and the pain of uncertainty', *Perceptual and Motor Skills*, 33, 3. Available from: https://journals.sagepub.com/doi/abs/10.2466/pms.1971.33.3f.1195 [Accessed on 21 August 2024].

4   UCL News (2016) 'Uncertainty can cause more stress than inevitable pain', 29 March. Available from: www.ucl.ac.uk/news/2016/mar/uncertainty-can-cause-more-stress-inevitable-pain [Accessed on 21 August 2024].

5   Hirsh, Jacob B. and Inzlicht, Michael (2008) 'The devil you know: Neuroticism predicts neural response to uncertainty', *Psychological Science*, 19(10): 962–7, doi: 10.1111/j.1467-9280.2008.02183.x.

6   Pentland, Alex (Sandy) (2008) *Honest Signals: How They Shape Our World*, Cambridge, MA: The MIT Press. Available from: https://direct.mit.edu/books/book/2037/Honest-SignalsHow-They-Shape-Our-World [Accessed on 21 August 2024].

7   Although Skinner's book was not well received in his lifetime, his ideas are still alive and kicking. I heard them as I interviewed a famous American psychologist who described less than purely humans as 'the enemy'.

8   You can find Skinner's seminal text, *Beyond Freedom and Dignity*, at: https://archive.org/stream/Beyond_Freedom_and_Dignity/Beyond%20Freedom%20&%20Dignity%20-%20Skinner_djvu.txt

9   Christakis, Nicholas A. and Fowler, James H. (2013) 'Social contagion theory: Examining dynamic social networks and human behavior', *Statistics in Medicine*, 32(4): 10.1002/sim.5408. Available from: www.ncbi.nlm.nih.gov/pmc/articles/PMC3830455 [Accessed on 21 August 2024].

10 Pentland, Alex (2014) 'The death of individuality: What really governs your actions?' *New Scientist*, 222(2963): 30–1. doi: 10.1016/S0262-4079(14)60684-9.

[11] There is a mounting literature taking apart some of the key 'findings' of behavioural economics, of which this is but one example: Hreha, Jason (no date) 'The death of behavioral economics', Behavioral Science blog. Available from: www.thebehavioralscientist.com/articles/the-death-of-behavioral-economics [Accessed on 21 August 2024]. At *The New York Review*, Tamsin Shaw has also been an eloquent sceptic: Shaw, Tamsin (2017) 'Invisible manipulators of your mind', *The New York Review*, 20 April. Available from: www.nybooks.com/articles/2017/04/20/kahneman-tversky-invisible-mind-manipulators [Accessed on 21 August 2024].

[12] O'Kane, Josh (2022) *Sideways: The City Google Couldn't Buy*, Vancouver, BC: Random House, p 50.

[13] O'Kane's book also contains a hilarious illustration of what happens when just a few things go wrong – see pp 51–54.

[14] Ibid, pp 182, 183.

[15] Mance, Henry (2022) 'Carlo Rovelli: "Science is not just about writing equations. It's about reconceptualising the world"', *Financial Times*, 26 September. Available from: www.ft.com/content/a67761c1-0cda-4782-b89e-610abd3104d2 [Accessed on 21 August 2024].

[16] Jackson, Maggie (2023) *Uncertain: The Wisdom and Wonder of Being Unsure*, Amherst, NY: Prometheus Books.

[17] Buck, Louisa (2022) 'Art down to the atom: Cornelia Parker discusses her work with a quantum physicist', *The Art Newspaper*, 16 September. Available from: www.theartnewspaper.com/2022/09/16/art-by-the-atom-cornelia-parker-discusses-her-work-with-a-quantum-physicist [Accessed on 21 August 2024].

[18] Rovelli, Carlo (2018) *There Are Places in the World Where Rules Are Less Important Than Kindness*. London: Allen Lane.

[19] The same is true of teamwork or any kind of collaboration – what makes the difference isn't individual capabilities, but the quality of exchange *between* individuals. See Heffernan, Margaret (2014) *A Bigger Prize: Why No One Wins Unless Everyone Wins*. London: Simon & Schuster; Heffernan, Margaret (2015) 'Forget the pecking order at work', TEDWomen. Available from: www.ted.com/talks/margaret_heffernan_forget_the_pecking_order_at_work [Accessed on 21 August 2024].

[20] While there has been much discussion of late about the need to foster 'psychological safety' in the workplace, there are limits to what this can achieve. Anyone on a gig economy contract won't feel safe; their precariousness is endemic to the business model. Nobody with a large mortgage feels safe when inflation is high and interest rates are rising. Even the finest leaders can't make the reality of economic volatility go away.

[21] I'm grateful to Markham Heid whose article on this subject explained my own restlessness to me: Heid, Markham (2024) 'The life-ruining power of routines', *FT Magazine*, 9/10 March, pp 14–16.

[22] Szablowski, Witold (2014) *Dancing Bears: True Stories of People Nostalgic for Life under Tyranny*, New York: Penguin Books.

23 McDermott, Amy (2021) 'What was the first "art"? How would we know?' *PNAS: Proceedings of the National Academy of Sciences*, 118(44): e2117561118, doi: 10.1073/pnas.2117561118. There is even an emerging argument that the earliest art, such as that found in the Chauvet Cave, was useful, in the sense that it drove the invention of increasingly sophisticated tools. See Morris, Michael (2024) *Tribal: How the Cultural Instincts that Divide Us Can Help Bring Us Together*, London: Penguin, p 61.

Chapter 1

1 Woolf, Virginia (1967) *Mrs Dalloway*, London: Penguin Books, p 6.

2 Oppezzo, Marily and Schwartz, Daniel L. (2014) 'Give your ideas some legs: The positive effect of walking on creative thinking', *Journal of Experimental Psychology, Learning, Memory, and Cognition*, 40(4): 1142–52. Available from: https://pubmed.ncbi.nlm.nih.gov/24749966 [Accessed on 21 August 2024].

3 Jackson, Maggie (2023) *Uncertain: The Wisdom and Wonder of Being Unsure*, Amherst, NY: Prometheus Books. This is an excellent look at the science that supports the value of uncertainty.

4 Kaplan, Stephen and Berman, Marc G. (2010) 'Directed attention as a common resource for executive functioning and self-regulation', *Perspectives on Psychological Science*, 5(1): 43–57. Available from: www.jstor.org/stable/41613309 [Accessed on 21 August 2024].

5 BBC Four (2019) *Searching for Sam – Adrian Dunbar on Samuel Beckett*. Available from: www.bbc.co.uk/mediacentre/proginfo/2019/53/adrian-dunbar-on-samuel-beckett [Accessed on 21 August 2024].

6 Tóibín, Colm (2018) 'The aristocracy's Swann Song', *The New York Review*, 11 October.

7 *The Paris Review* (2023) 'Olga Tokarczuk, The art of fiction, No. 258', interviewed by Marta Figlerowicz, Issue 243. Available from www.theparisreview/org/interviews/7968/the-art-of-fiction-no-258-olga-tokarczuk [Accessed on 5 August 2024].

8 Grey, Tobias (2018) 'Olga Tokarczuk's book *Flights* is taking off', *The New York Times*, 9 August. Available from: www.nytimes.com/2018/08/09/books/olga-tokarczuk-flights-booker.html [Accessed on 5 August 2024].

9 Woolf, Virginia (1926) 'How should one read a book? Read as if one were writing it', *The Yale Review*, Autumn. Available from: https://yalereview.org/article/virginia-woolf-essay-how-should-read-book [Accessed on 5 August 2024].

10 Woolf, Virginia (1959) 'How should one read a book? Read as if one were writing it', in *The Common Reader, Second Series*, London: The Hogarth Press Ltd.

11 Ibid.

12 'Modern Novels (Joyce)', Reading notes, Monk's House Papers, University of Sussex. Quotes in Hermione Lee's biography *Virginia Woolf*, London: Vintage Books, 1997.

13 Mead, Rebecca (2017) 'Margaret Atwood, the prophet of dystopia', *The New Yorker*, 10 April. Available from: www.newyorker.com/

magazine/2017/04/17/margaret-atwood-the-prophet-of-dystopia [Accessed 5 August 2024].

[14] This also explains why the journey to a new destination always seems so much longer than the return – because there is so much that is new to process.

[15] When a *New York Times* journalist tried out AI travel itinerary apps, he visited all the obvious sites; what became most striking were the interventions he made in its planning and the fact that at no point does he appear to have spoken to a single Norwegian: Yeğinsu, Ceylan (2024) 'My first trip to Norway, with AI as a guide', *The New York Times*, 26 June. Available from: www.nytimes.com/2024/06/26/travel/norway-artficial-intelligence-planners.html?utm_source=substack&utm_medium=email [Accessed 4 September 2024].

[16] Geertz, Clifford (1998) 'Deep hanging out', *The New York Review*, 22 October. Available from: www.nybooks.com/articles/1998/10/22/deep-hanging-out [Accessed on 5 August 2024]. It's probably due to this review that the phrase 'deep hanging out' is often misattributed to Geertz himself, although he quoted the term when describing James Clifford's book *Routes*. Another seminal anthropologist was full of praise for the process – Pierre Clastres wrote, 'I had only to look around me at the daily life: even with a minimum of attention I could always discover something new.'

[17] Menon, Vinod (2023) '20 years of the default mode network: A review and synthesis', *Neuron*, 111(6): 2469–87, doi: 10.1016/j.neuron.2023.04.023.

[18] Spurling, Hilary (1998) *The Unknown Matisse: A Life of Henri Matisse*, London: Penguin Books, p 59.

[19] Jackson, Maggie (2023) *Uncertain: The Wisdom and Wonder of Being Unsure*, Guildford, CT: Prometheus Books.

Chapter 2

[1] Mitter, Siddhartha (2024) 'Steve McQueen, on a different wavelength', *The New York Times*, 10 May. Available from: www.nytimes.com/2024/05/10/arts/design/steve-mcqueen-filmmaker-art-dia-beacon-bass.html [Accessed on 11 August 2024].

[2] Murakami, Haruki (2022) *Novelist as a Vocation*, translated from the Japanese by Philip Gabriel and Ted Goose, New York: Vintage Books.

[3] *The Paris Review* (2018) 'Frederick Wiseman, The art of documentary No. 1', interviewed by Lola Peploe, Issue 226. Available from: www.theparisreview.org/interviews/7210/the-art-of-documentary-no-1-frederick-wiseman [Accessed on 21 August 2024].

[4] Kavanagh, Patrick (1967) *Collected Pruse*, London: MacGibbon & Kee.

[5] There have, of course, been groups of artists working together with a shared ethos: the pre-Raphaelite Brotherhood, the Dadaists, Futurists, Impressionists etc. Many of these exhibited together. But individual artists within these groups still signed their works individually, and many went on to build strong separate identities. They might more properly be called movements as they did not operate as collectives. It's worth saying, however,

that many collectives today define themselves in a range of different ways, and there remains huge contention about which are true collectives.

6 Tate Talks (2017) 'Lubaina Himid in conversation with Maria Balshaw'. Available from: www.youtube.com/watch?v=edsXUqhnAOA [Accessed on 21 August 2024].

7 Murakami, Haruki (2022) *Novelist as a Vocation*, translated from the Japanese by Philip Gabriel and Ted Goose, New York: Vintage Books.

8 *The Paris Review* (2023) 'Olga Tokarczuk, The art of fiction, No. 258', interviewed by Marta Figlerowicz, Issue 243, Spring, pp 199–228. www.theparisreview.org/interviews/7968/the-art-of-fiction-no-258-olga-tokarczuk

9 McGlone, Rosanna (ed) (2023) *The Process of Poetry: From First Draft to Final Poem: Curated Interviews with Award-Winning Poets*, New Mills: Fly on the Wall Press.

10 This isn't for lack of trying. But it's virtually impossible in social sciences and in the arts to do large, controlled experiments, where conditions can be carefully calibrated and stable. The external context of the real – mood, politics, people – is too complex and differentiated.

11 Barry, Sebastian (2022) *The Lives of the Saints*, London: Faber & Faber.

12 *The Paris Review* (1984) 'James Baldwin, the art of fiction No. 78', interviewed by Jordan Elgrably, Issue 91, spring. Available at: www.theparisreview.org/interviews/2994/the-art-of-fiction-no-78-james-baldwin [Accessed 7 October 2024].

Chapter 3

1 Kavanagh, Patrick (1967) *Collected Pruse*, London: MacGibbon & Kee.

2 Bowling, Frank (2022) *Penumbral Light*, Zurich: Hauser & Wirth Publishers.

3 Belz, Corinna (director) (2011) *Gerhard Richter Painting* [film], zero one film.

4 The BBC made a film about the event that is sometimes available on iPlayer: www.bbc.co.uk/programmes/b083bk7n

5 Kahn, Ashley (2002) *Kind of Blue: The Making of the Miles Davis Masterpiece*, London: Granta Books.

6 Ibid.

7 The comments are from an edition of BBC Radio 4's *Soul Music*, first broadcast on 30 September 2008: www.bbc.co.uk/sounds/play/b00dnjrn

8 Kahn, Ashley (2002) *Kind of Blue: The Making of the Miles Davis Masterpiece*, London: Granta Books.

9 *The Paris Review* (2023) 'Olga Tokarczuk, The art of fiction No. 258', interviewed by Marta Figlerowicz, Issue 243. Available from: www.theparisreview.org/interviews/7968/the-art-of-fiction-no-258-olga-tokarczuk?mc_cid=fba1e05122&mc_eid=4d88d1aeb7 [Accessed 5 September 2024].

10 *The Paris Review* (2018) *The Writer's Chapbook: A Compendium of Fact, Opinion, Wit, and Advice from 'The Paris Review' Interviews*, New York: The Paris Review.

[11] See https://mahlerfoundation.org/mahler/compositions/symphony-no-1/symphony-no-1-history. The same might be said of Beethoven's only opera, *Fidelio*, still cherished for all its ostensible flaws.

[12] I've been unable to find the original cartoon, which I remember since I first read it, so I was relieved to find this account of it here: www.bewilderingstories.com/issue393/ch393resp_intentional.html

[13] This comes from the docent's guide to the 'Lost Threads' exhibition at the Holburne Museum in Bath in February 2024.

[14] Graef delivered the *Manifesto* to BAFTA on 12 May 2014 (www.bafta.org/heritage/features/a-tribute-to-roger-graef), which was subsequently repeated it his memorial service in London at Broadcasting House on 14 July 2023.

[15] Himid, Lubaina and Smith, Marlene (2024) 'Marlene Smith and Lubaina Himid on friendship and collaboration', *Frieze*, 244, Interviews, 5 June. Available from: www.frieze.com/article/lubaina-himid-marlene-smith-interview-244 [Accessed on 11 August 2024].

[16] *The Paris Review* (1969) 'Writers at work: 4th series', interview with Peter Buckman and William Fifield.

[17] When the psychotherapist Anthony Storr asked Agatha Christie how much time elapsed between finishing a book and starting a new one, she said: 'Enough time for a cup of tea'. It was his belief that this compulsion to write was in some way pathological, a form of avoidance. I do not think that is what Kinch is describing.

[18] *The Paris Review* (1984) 'James Baldwin, The art of fiction, No. 78', interviewed by Jordan Elgrably, Issue 91. Available from: www.theparisreview.org/interviews/2994/the-art-of-fiction-no-78-james-baldwin [Accessed on 11 August 2024].

[19] Heaney, Seamus (1995) *The Redress of Poetry: Oxford Lectures*, London: Faber & Faber.

[20] Wilson, Edmund (1983) 'An account of *Peter Grimes* from "London in midsummer"', in P. Brett (ed) *Benjamin Britten: Peter Grimes*, Cambridge: Cambridge University Press, Chapter 10.

[21] Auden, W.H. (1939) 'In Memory of W.B. Yeats'.

Chapter 4

[1] Jowett, Patrick (2023) 'Entries to GCSE arts exams hit new low', *Arts Professional*, 30 August. Available from: www.artsprofessional.co.uk/news/entries-gcse-arts-exams-hit-new-low [Accessed on 7 October 2024].

[2] Department for Education (2019) 'English Baccalaureate (EBacc) Guidance' [updated 20 August]. Available from: www.gov.uk/government/publications/english-baccalaureate-ebacc/english-baccalaureate-ebacc [Accessed on 20 August 2024].

[3] The EBacc isn't compulsory, but the government's goal for students doing it was 75 per cent by 2022 and 90 per cent by 2025 (see www.williamfarr.lincs.sch.uk/ks4-english-baccalaureate).

4   Wilcock, David (2020) 'Culture Secretary Oliver Dowden apologies for "crass" advert suggesting a ballerina retrains in cyber-security after Twitter outrage – despite it coming from a scheme launched BEFORE coronavirus', *Mail Online*, 12 October. Available from: www.dailymail.co.uk/news/article-8831037/Culture-Secretary-apologises-crass-advert-suggesting-ballerina-retrains-cyber-security.html [Accessed on 20 August 2024]. Sadly, I know one student who followed the advice of the exam. Having secured his cybersecurity degree, he has no interest at all in working in the area, and now feels he wasted his time and money.

5   Jowett, Patrick (2021) 'Creative degree applications rise as university arts funding halved', *Arts Professional*, 22 July. Available from: www.artsprofessional.co.uk/news/creative-degree-applications-rise-university-arts-funding-halved [Accessed on 20 August 2024].

6   This mistake is not at all unique to education; it is also pervasive in performance management systems at work, which routinely prioritize input (hours of work) over output (the value of what is made). It's common, too, to measure *what* got done (hitting the sales target) over *how* it gets done (by misselling products to customers who didn't want them) even when how targets are met can determine reputation, loyalty and even survival.

7   See the American Academy of Arts & Sciences' Humanities Indicators (www.amacad.org/humanities-indicators).

8   Kisida, Brian and Bowen, Daniel H. (2019) 'New evidence of the benefits of arts education', Commentary, 12 February, Brookings. Available from: www.brookings.edu/articles/new-evidence-of-the-benefits-of-arts-education [Accessed on 20 August 2024].

9   Ruppert, Sandra S. (2006) *Critical Evidence: How the Arts Benefit Student Performance*, National Assembly of State Arts Agencies. Available from: https://files.eric.ed.gov/fulltext/ED529766.pdf [Accessed on 20 August 2024]; Mehta, Jal (2017) 'Schools already have good learning, just not where you think', *Education Week*, 8 February.

10 I am very grateful to Dublin City University for sharing their research into transversal skills with me.

11 See www.oecd-ilibrary.org/docserver/b3a46696-en.pdf

12 See www.oecd.org/pisa/innovation/creative-thinking

13 See www.oecd-ilibrary.org/docserver/b3a46696-en.pdf

14 Jackson, Maggie (2023) *Uncertain: The Wisdom and Wonder of Being Unsure*, Amherst, NY: Prometheus Books. Jackson also cites important research done by Mary Helen Immordino-Yang, showing that what we consider to be wakeful rest engages the brain's default mode, which is important for imagining the future and for feeling social emotions with moral connotations. 'People with stronger default mode connectivity at rest score higher on measures of cognitive abilities like divergent thinking, reading comprehension and memory.' See: Immordino-Yang, Mary Helen, Christodoulou, Joanna and Singh, Vanessa (2012) 'Rest is not idleness: Implications of the brain's default mode for human development and education', *Perspectives on Psychological Science*, 7(4): 352–64. Available from: www.researchgate.net/

publication/228332491_Rest_Is_Not_Idleness_Implications_of_the_ Brain%27s_Default_Mode_for_Human_Development_and_Education [Accessed on 5 September 2024].

[15] The field of self-determination theory was pioneered by Edward Deci and Richard Ryan in the mid-1980s; see Ryan, Richard M. and Deci, Edward L. (2000) 'Self-determination theory and the facilitation of intrinsic motivation, social development, and well-being', *American Psychologist*, 55(1): 68–78. Available from: https://selfdeterminationtheory.org/SDT/ documents/2000_RyanDeci_SDT.pdf [Accessed on 20 August 2024]. For an excellent examination of intrinsic and extrinsic motivation as it plays out in life and work, Daniel Pink's book *Drive* is an excellent summary of the academic research, and a thoughtful, imaginative application of it: Pink, Daniel H. (2011) *Drive: The Surprising Truth about What Motivates Us*, London: Canongate Books Ltd.

[16] Harvey, Adrian (2016) *Funding Arts and Culture in a Time of Austerity*, London: New Local Government Network. Available from: www.artscouncil.org.uk/ sites/default/files/download-file/Funding%20Arts%20and%20Culture%20 in%20a%20time%20of%20Austerity%20%28Adrian%20Harvey%29.pdf [Accessed on 20 August 2024].

[17] Harrison, Phil (2024) '"The business is no longer sustainable": The inside story of how Tory cuts devastated the arts', *The Guardian*, 29 June. Available from: www.theguardian.com/culture/article/2024/jun/29/what-14-years-of-tory-rule-have-done-to-the-arts [Accessed on 5 September 2024]. In a public talk in Bath on 12 June 2024, James Shapiro discussed political attitudes to the National Endowment for the Arts.

[18] For 2024 BBC research, see https://mapping-museums.bbk. ac.uk/2024/03/20/new-data-on-uk-museum-closure-2000-2024-governance-and-region and Lynch, Paul, Tomas, Pilar and Hattenstone, Alix (2024) 'Public libraries in "crisis" as councils cut services', BBC News, 3 September. Available from: www.bbc.co.uk/news/articles/cn9lexplel5o [Accessed on 5 September 2024].

[19] Heller, Nathan (2023) 'The end of the English Major', *The New Yorker*, 6 March. Available from: www.newyorker.com/magazine/2023/03/06/the-end-of-the-english-major [Accessed on 20 August 2024]. Also, in a public talk in Bath in the UK in June 2024, James Shapiro argued that in the USA the Republicans were seeking to eliminate the National Endowment for the Arts (NEA).

[20] DACS research, July 2024 (see www.dacs.org.uk/advocacy/freelance-labour).

[21] Kisida, Brian and Bowen Daniel H. (2019) 'New evidence of the benefits of arts education', Commentary, 12 February, Brookings. Available from: www. brookings.edu/articles/new-evidence-of-the-benefits-of-arts-education [Accessed on 20 August 2024].

[22] Automotive industries: £13.3 billion in 2022; pharmaceutical industries: £65.5 billion in 2022; aerospace £16.7 billion. See, respectively, Panjwani, Abbas (2023) 'Automotive industry in the UK debate', Research Briefing,

15 September. Available from: https://commonslibrary.parliament.uk/research-briefings/cdp-2023-0189 [Accessed on 5 September 2024]; www.statista.com/statistics/293591/pharmaceutical-goods-wholesalers-total-turnover-in-the-united-kingdom; International Trade Administration (2023) 'Aerospace and Defense', Country Commercial Guides, 3 November. Available from: www.trade.gov/country-commercial-guides/united-kingdom-aerospace-and-defense [Accessed on 5 September 2024].

23 Fancourt, Daisy, Bone, J.K., Bu, F., Mak, H.W. and Bradbury, A. (2023) *The Impact of Arts and Cultural Engagement on Population Health: Findings from Major Cohort Studies in the UK and USA 2017–2022*, London: University College London. Available from: https://sbbresearch.org/wp-content/uploads/2023/03/Arts-and-population-health-FINAL-March-2023.pdf [Accessed on 20 August 2024]. There is a mountain of research into this subject, but this report is an excellent summary.

24 Mar, Raymond A. and Oatley, Keith (2008) 'The function of fiction is the abstraction and simulation of social experience', *Perspectives on Psychological Science*, 3: 173–92. doi:10.1111/j.1745-6924.2008.00073.x.

25 Williams Woolley, Anita, Chabris, Christopher F., Pentland, Alex, Hashmi, Nada and Malone, Thomas W. (2010) 'Evidence for a collective intelligence factor in the performance of human groups', *Science*, 330(6004): 686–8. doi: 10.1126/science.1193147.

26 Tamir, Diana I., Bricker, Andrew B., Dodell-Feder, David and Mitchell, Jason P. (2016) 'Reading fiction and reading minds: The role of simulation in the default network', *Social Cognitive and Affective Neuroscience*, 11(2): 215–24. doi: 10.1093/scan/nsv114.

27 See https://fastfamiliar.com/about

28 De Meyer, Kris, 'Shutdown! Using immersive theatre to assess people's reactions to nationwide power failure', King's College London. Available from: www.crforum.co.uk/research-and-resources/shutdown-using-experiential-learning-and-scenario-planning [Accessed on 28 October 2024].

29 In many ways, this reflects learning from citizens' assemblies. We know from these that listening to lived experience from peers, not pundits, encouraged members of the Irish citizens' assemblies to think more discursively about the issues before them and, in many instances, to change their minds.

30 Dolev, Jacqueline C., Friedlaender, Linda and Braverman, Irwin M. (2001) 'Use of fine art to enhance visual diagnostic skills', *Journal of the American Medical Association*, 286(9): 1020–1, doi: 10.1001/jama.286.9.1020. See also https://arthistory.utdallas.edu/medicine

31 Chisholm, Margaret S. and Kelly-Hedrick, Margot (2021) 'How visual arts-based education can promote clinical excellence', *Academic Medicine*, 96(8): 110–4, doi: 10.1097/ACM.0000000000003862. VTS are guided by three basic questions: (1) What's going on in this picture? (2) What do you see that makes you say that? (3) What more can we find?

Chapter 5

1. hooks, bell (1994) *Outlaw Culture: Resisting Representations*, London: Routledge.
2. Richtarik, Marilynn J. (1994) *Acting between the Lines: The Field Day Theatre Company and Irish Cultural Politics 1980–1984*, Oxford: Clarendon Press, p 12.
3. Ibid, p 26, quoting an Editorial in the *Irish Press*.
4. Ibid, p 35.
5. Foster, Roy F. (2014) *Vivid Faces: The Revolutionary Generation in Ireland 1890–1923*, London: Allen Lane.
6. Ibid.
7. Heaney, Seamus (1983) *An Open Letter*, Field Day Pamphlet 2, Derry: Field Day Company Ltd.
8. Heaney, Seamus (2018) *The Cure at Troy: A Version of Sophocles' Philoctetes*, London: Faber & Faber.
9. *The Paris Review* (2000) 'Derek Mahon, The art of poetry No. 82', interviewed by Eamon Grennan, Issue 154. Available from: www.theparisreview. org/interviews/732/the-art-of-poetry-no-82-derek-mahon [Accessed on 20 August 2024].
10. This line appears in his poem 'In Memory of W.B. Yeats'.
11. Gilot, Françoise and Lake, Carlton (1990) *Life with Picasso*, London: Virago, p 116.
12. Freedberg, Catherine B. (1986) *The Spanish Pavilion at the Paris World's Fair*, New York and London: Garland Publishing. Available from: https://archive.org/details/spanishpaviliona0000free/page/n5/mode/2up [Accessed on 20 August 2024].
13. Piper, Myfanwy (1937) *The Painter's Object*, London: Curwen Press.
14. van Hensbergen, Gijs (2004) *Guernica: The Biography of a Twentieth Century Icon*, London: Bloomsbury.
15. Attlee, James (2017) *Guernica: Painting the End of the World*, London: Head of Zeus, p 201.
16. Wilson, Owen (2008) 'Interview with Tony Shafrazi', *Interview* magazine, 24 November. Available from: www.interviewmagazine.com/fashion/tony-shafrazi [Accessed on 3 September 2024].
17. Ringgold, Faith (2018) 'In conversation', Tate Modern Talks_Lectures, 5 July. Available from: www.tate.org.uk/whats-on/tate-modern/soul-nation-art-age-black-power/artists-talk-faith-ringgold [Accessed on 20 August 2024]. The picture, and Ringgold's comments on it, can be seen at www.tate.org.uk/tate-etc/issue-40-summer-2017/soul-nation-artists-faith-ringgold-jack-whitten-lorraine-ogrady-betye-saar-dawoud-bey
18. Ibid.
19. Vasilogambros, Matt (2018) 'After Parkland, states pass 50 new gun-control laws', *Stateline*, 2 August. Available from: https://stateline.org/2018/08/02/after-parkland-states-pass-50-new-gun-control-laws [Accessed on 20 August 2024].
20. Roy Cohn's panel reads 'Bully. Coward. Victim'.

21 Quotes and details from 'Souls Grown Deep like the Rivers, Black artists from the American South', 2023 exhibition, Royal Academy of Arts (see www.royalacademy.org.uk/exhibition/souls-grown-deep).

22 Bourton, Lucy (2021) 'How the banner of Greenham Common Women's Peace Camp fought horror with beauty', *It's Nice That*, 26 August. Available from: www.itsnicethat.com/features/women-for-peace-greenham-common-banners-four-corners-thalia-campbell-art-publication-260821 [Accessed on 20 August 2024].

23 Corbett, Sarah (2019) 'How a gentle protest with hand-embroidered hankies helped bring higher wages for retail employees', Ideas.Ted.Com, 24 January. Available from: https://ideas.ted.com/how-a-gentle-protest-with-hand-embroidered-hankies-helped-bring-higher-wages-for-retail-employees [Accessed on 20 August 2024].

24 De Meyer, Kris, Coren, Emily, McCaffrey, Mark and Slean, Cheryl (2021) 'Transforming the stories we tell about climate change: From "issue" to "action"', *Environmental Research, Letters*, 16: 015002, doi: 10.1088/1748-9326/abcd5a.

25 Akhmatova, A. (2006) *Selected Poems*, translated by Richard McKane, Hexham: Bloodaxe Books.

26 Berlin, Isaiah (1997) 'Anna Akhmatova: A Memoir', in Roberta Reeder (ed) *The Complete Poems of Anna Akhmatova*, translated by Judith Hemschemeyer, Boston, MA: Zephyr Press, pp 35–55.

27 Akhmatova, A. (2006) *Selected Poems*, translated by Richard McKane, Hexham: Bloodaxe Books.

28 Ibid.

29 Steiner, George (1998) *After Babel: Aspects of Language and Translation*, Oxford: Oxford University Press.

30 Eichler, Jeremy (2023) *Time's Echo*, London: Faber & Faber, p 258.

31 Eichler, Jeremy (2023) 'Shostakovich's musical home for conscience, revisited at a time of need', *The Boston Globe*, 5 May. Available from: www.bostonglobe.com/2023/05/05/arts/shostakovichs-musical-home-conscience-revisited-time-need [Accessed on 20 August 2024].

32 Jeremy Eichler's wonderful book, *Time's Echo*, is brilliant on the theme of music and politics, and also with regard to Strauss, Schoenberg and Britten. See Eichler, Jeremy (2023) *Time's Echo: Music, Memory and the Second World War*, London: Faber & Faber.

33 From the 2015 film *What Happened, Miss Simone?*, a 2015 American biographical documentary film about Nina Simone directed by Liz Garbus.

34 Ibid, at around 1:02:11 from the end.

35 The documentary *CALL NINA!*, directed by Lamin Daniel Jadama, shows the development of this show, its performances around the world and Bushell-Mingo's work in Sweden, the USA and the UK.

36 Gilbert, Ben (2016) 'Kendrick Lamar's civil rights anthem "Alright" almost didn't happen', *Business Insider*, 25 October. Available from: www.businessinsider.com/kendrick-lamar-alright-2016-10?r=US&IR=T [Accessed on 20 August 2024].

Index